FINISHING THE TASK

World Evangelism in Our Generation

Compiled by
JOHN E. KYLE
Foreword by
RALPH D. WINTER

Regal Books

A Division of GL Publications
Ventura, California, U.S.A.

Published by Regal Books
A Division of GL Publications
Ventura, California 93006
Printed in U.S.A.

Library of Congress Cataloging-in-Publication Data.

Finishing the task.

Includes bibliographies.
1. Missions. 2. Evangelistic work. I. Kyle, John E., 1926-
BV2061.F56   1987   266'.099'04   87-28341
ISBN 0-8307-1251-8

2 3 4 5 6 7 8 9 10 / 91 90 89 88

Contents

*"There are moments in our lives when we make massive changes
of direction in a short period of time. These can be called
turntable moments."*

*"No other single subject has ever captured my mind like this one.
The year 2000 means 100 times more to me than it did
earlier this year."*

*"Many have called the SVM the greatest student missionary
movement in history . . . . The Student Volunteers demonstrated
consecration; they were ready to sacrifice for their Lord."*

List of Contributors

DAVID BRYANT has been with InterVarsity Missions since 1976 and serves as the Minister At Large for InterVarsity Missions. He is the author of *In the Gap* and *With Concerts of Prayer* and introduced the concept of Christians becoming "World Christians" on campuses throughout the U.S. David serves on the National Prayer Committee and has been a pastor of a church in Kent, Ohio. He and his wife Robyne have three children from India, Adam, Bethany and Benjamin. They reside in Madison, Wisconsin.

ELIZABETH CRIDLAND is the representative for Africa Inland Mission for the Mid-Atlantic states. She served over 40 years in Africa with both the Africa Inland Mission and Sudan Interior Mission, responsible for many churches being planted in Africa. She helped start the Bible Alliance Mission on her return to the U.S. when most people would have retired. She is a gifted speaker well loved by students of this generation. She and her colleague of over 40 years, Mary Beam, make their home in Greenville, South Carolina.

DAN HARRISON is the associate director of InterVarsity Missions. He has served as the executive director of English Language Institute for China, as well as a vice president of Wycliffe Bible Translators. He has been a member of Wycliffe Bible Translators for 23 years serving for many years in Papua New Guinea. He and his wife Shelby have four children, Paula, Melody, Holly and Tonya. The Harrisons reside in Madison, Wisconsin.

JAYSON D. KYLE is a missionary to Mexico with Mission to the World of the Presbyterian Church in America. He has served in Papua New Guinea with Wycliffe Bible Translators and also as coordinator of personnel for Mission to the World. He and his wife Maureen have three children, Jennifer, Jeffery and Amy. They reside in Mexico City.

GORDON MacDONALD was the pastor of Grace Chapel in Lexington, Massachusetts. He has traveled in Africa, Asia, Europe and Latin America. He served as the chairman of the board of World Vision International and as president of InterVarsity Christian Fellowship U.S.A. in addition to writing several books. He and his wife Gail have two children, Mark and Kristen.

PAUL McKAUGHAN most recently served as the coordinator of Mission to the World of the Presbyterian Church of America. He served with the Billy Graham Evangelistic Association in Brazil and also O.C. Ministries for several terms. He was the associate director of the Billy Graham

Crusade in Rio de Janeiro in the mid-1970s. He currently serves as the associate international director of the Lausanne Continuing Committee for World Evangelization. He and his wife Joanne have three children, Don, Doug and Debbie.

H. WILBERT NORTON, SR. was a missionary to the Belgian Congo (now Zaire) and has served as president of Trinity College and Trinity Evangelical Divinity School and dean of the Wheaton Graduate School. He was the founding principal of the Jos Theological Seminary in Nigeria and presently is the chaplain to International Scholars at Wheaton College Graduate School and executive director of the Committee to Assist Ministry Education Overseas. He resides in Wheaton, Illinois with his wife Colene. They have three sons, Wilbert, Jr., Seth and Peter.

J. CHRISTY WILSON, JR. was a missionary to Afghanistan for 22 years. He eventually pastored an English-speaking church in Kabul, Afghanistan, which was allowed to be constructed due to a visit by President Eisenhower and his request to the king. Wilson is a graduate of Princeton Theological Seminary and presently serves as the professor of missions at Gordon-Conwell Theological Seminary. He and his wife Betty have three children, Nancy, Chris and Martin.

RALPH D. WINTER is the founder and director of the U.S. Center for World Mission in Pasadena, California. He served in Guatemala as a missionary for several years with the Presbyterian Church in the United States of America's Board of Foreign Missions. He also was professor of history and missions at the School of World Mission of Fuller Theological Seminary for several years. He has been largely responsible for the missions strategy directed toward outreach to the "Unreached Peoples." He and his wife Roberta have four children, Patricia, Linda, Becky and Beth.

Foreword

No event in my lifetime, short of the return of Christ, could possibly compete with the immense portent of an almost unknown series of events in the past century, which this book now explodes into view.

The key characters in that potent cast include huge, chunky Dwight L. Moody, the unlettered, almost backwoods evangelist whose humility and spiritual power shook his whole generation—and the entire English-speaking world—like no other.

Then there is the scholarly pastor, A. T. Pierson, whose global mission knowledge had no parallel. And John R. Mott, the tall, handsome student leader, who at an early stage was a bit uppity but very capable and soon highly dedicated. And there are so many more.

But what were they up to? That is what is spellbinding! First the totally unpredictable breakthrough of this Moody fellow at ultra snobbish Cambridge University. And the "sailing" of the Cambridge Seven—which fell like a bombshell in the upper strata of all England. And the reverberations in this country—but I am not going to scoop this story.

Sufficient to say they plotted to "Finish the task" by the year 1900 (note the date!). They knew what they were doing. What they planned was feasible. Today it is 20 times as feasible—"by the year 2000." They failed then because the children of the Kingdom did not push forward in obedience. What then shall we do today? That is the unavoidable point of this book.

Will you try to avoid it? Then don't read this book. Will you face the rupture of personal priorities the timetable of history will inevitably impose upon all who take it seriously? Can you "drink the cup" of the ordeal of finally, definitively exchanging your American passion for a new career, to a much more freeing passion to believe and obey within a cause? Then this book is for you!

—Ralph D. Winter

Publisher's Preface

Is there something Christians today have to learn from the inauspicious beginnings of student missionary movements 100 years ago, or even 50 years ago? Don't we have unparalleled opportunities and enormous resources of money and technology to spread the good news of Jesus Christ to the whole world? What more could there be?

Well, there's more, and *Finishing the Task* serves to remind the whole Body of Christ there's much we can learn from past student movements.

This book has moved and challenged me as few others have. And to be honest, I've had to ask myself why.

The one hundredth anniversary of the Student Volunteer Movement (SVM) and the fiftieth anniversary of the Student Foreign Missions Fellowship (SFMF) are celebrated within the pages of *Finishing the Task*, a compilation of messages presented in 1986 at the Ben Lippen Conference Center in North Carolina.

Although the messages were given to motivate students, they are of even greater importance for the students' parents, pastors and their church congregations to

read and understand, for they truly communicate the keys
that can unlock a mighty movement of the Spirit of God for
renewal of the Church and world evangelization.

What are those keys? Concerted prayer and material
support for the many volunteers God is raising up to "go"
in fulfillment of Matthew 28:19,20. And, interestingly, it
isn't only student volunteers God is calling, but whole families, business and professional people, blue collar workers
and retiring Americans, upon whose heart He has placed a
deep concern for the nearly 3 billion unreached people of
the world. Of special interest is a companion Regal book
being published simultaneously entitled *It's Never Too Late
to Say Yes,* by Keith Brown and John Hoover.

There's no doubt missionaries are needed to go out as
never before, but they cannot go unless they are sent by
the Church with strong prayer and financial support. As
those who can't go pray for and support those who can go,
whole congregations will take their eyes off themselves
and look instead to the great God who will give them a new
vision and sense of His indwelling presence.

In *Finishing the Task* Paul McKaughan points out,
"Prayer is one of the greatest means available to align ourselves with God's will. Somehow we get the idea that our
prayer life is a way to invent a future that God doesn't
know anything about . . . prayer lines up my will with
Christ's will."

Wil Norton notes, "The future of the student movement is directly associated with obedience in suffering.
That individual or organization only looking out for its own
interests and not the interests of others is doomed."

There are many signs that God is raising up a new
movement of committed young people, and older people,
too, to carry the gospel to the whole world before the next
century. This is an exciting time to be a Christian. We

need to ask ourselves, "Am I ready? Is my church ready?"

David Bryant says, "Today God has given us a very simple strategy for mission mobilization. First, you begin to live a life that shows you identify with God's heart for the whole world. Second, every chance you get you start giving a vision of God's heart for the world, and how that is all fulfilled through the person of Jesus who dwells in all His glory in the midst of us. Third, you look for those, even a handful at the beginning, who would be willing to gather with you to seek the face of God for both the inward and outward journey, for spiritual awakening and for the evangelization of the world."

Concerted prayer by God's people, sacrificial giving and living, and unbounded faith and obedience to the sovereign Lord are all God needs of us to bring about world evangelization in our generation! Are you willing to commit yourself and your church to that end?

I pray this book will serve to spark a missionary revival in me and my church, and in you and your church.

William T. Greig, Jr.

Introduction

Seldom does a group of college students gather to learn and discuss how fellow students over the past 100 years have been strategically used to reach the world for Christ. That's exactly what occurred on June 29-July 3, 1986 at the Ben Lippen Conference Center in Asheville, North Carolina. Not only did these men and women look back, they were encouraged to look to the present and the future to see how they could be used to help complete the task of world evangelization.

The occasion was the 100th anniversary of the Student Volunteer Movement, which in its heyday sent over 20,000 students to all parts of the world as missionaries. Also being celebrated was the 50th anniversary of the Student Foreign Missions Fellowship, which itself has thrust thousands of students into the mission fields of the world and is still in existence today.

We who were gathered at the Ben Lippen Conference were challenged and renewed afresh by messages brought from the Bible and experiences by men and women who have been greatly used of God and who at one time were college students themselves with a burning desire to serve Christ. With great privilege I witnessed the experienced adults passing on the baton of responsibility to young people eager to serve Christ overseas as missionaries.

A highlight of our time together was the evening we commissioned 23 college students to go to Amsterdam '86 to serve as stewards to the 6,000 evangelists from all over the world. It was a heart-searching evening as these young men and women were committed to the Lord through Scripture admonition by H. Wilbert Norton, Sr. and dedicated through prayer by Elizabeth Cridland to the service that lay ahead of them. We all rededicated our lives anew to the end of completing the task of reaching the 3 billion people around the world without Christ.

At the close of those strategic days, I realized that it was my further responsibility to not only plan and direct *SFMF 50th/SVM 100th Celebration,* but also to share with others on the printed page the messages that were used to challenge and encourage all of us who were present for those historic days at Ben Lippen. It was on that very site that 50 years ago the Student Foreign Missions Fellowship was founded.

I believe that we must do all that we can as Christians to enable the present generation of college students who are committed to going out as missionaries to places all around the world realize their missionary goals. Also, I continue to challenge college students who number in the thousands not to lay aside the burden the Lord Jesus Christ has given them to be involved in completing the task of reaching the lost with the gospel of Jesus Christ.

John E. Kyle, Director
InterVarsity Missions
InterVarsity Christian Fellowship, U.S.A.

1

The Turntable of Motivation
by
Gordon MacDonald

A little over a year ago, I was riding from Boston to New York on a train called the Metroliner. As the train wound its way from Boston, south to Rhode Island, and then to Mystic, Connecticut, it went very slowly through a railroad yard. Off to one side of the yard was an old rusty turntable.

Those of you who are old enough to remember the steam trains of Europe will know what I'm describing. Each day as the rail yard came to life, large engines and their tenders would crawl out on that turntable. A man would go to a little shed to push buttons and pull levers. This would cause the turntable to go around slowly until it faced another track; a change of direction had taken place.

I love sermon illustrations, and as I looked at that turntable I thought, there's got to be a spiritual principle behind what I'm seeing here. About eight miles down the track, I figured out what that illustration was: There are moments in our lives when we make massive changes of direction in a short period of time. These can be called turntable moments.

For example, a man has a massive heart attack. As he comes out of the intensive care unit, he says to his family, "I'll never be the same again. I'm going to use my time differently from now on." Or a woman has a bout with cancer. She comes out of successful surgery and says, "From now on things are going to be different."

A man is fired from a job he thought he had for life. Suddenly his security is gone. In the wake of that moment of rejection, there will be a turntable moment when he must make some swift and sweeping changes.

But there are also times when positive turntable moments take place. The Bible is full of examples. The conversion of Saul of Tarsus is a turntable event. The man was never the same after his experience on the road to Damascus (see Acts 9).

Throughout the Old Testament there are turntable moments. One of the most significant of these takes place in 1 Samuel 3. The boy Samuel was ministering to the Lord under the priest Eli. It's interesting that up to this point, Eli had the reputation for being a rotten father to his own children. Yet God trusts Eli with the mentoring of Samuel.

Now a word from the Lord was rare in those days. It had been a long time since, in the midst of all the religious activity at the Tabernacle at Shiloh, anyone had the satisfaction of a genuine communication from God.

Eli, whose eyesight had dimmed, was about 40 years old. One night while he and Samuel were lying down in the Temple, the Lord called, "Samuel."

Samuel ran to Eli and said, "You called me. Here I am." Eli told Samuel he had not called him and to go back to sleep.

When this happened twice more, Eli discerned that the Lord was calling the boy. So he told Samuel, "Go lie down and if He calls you, you shall say, 'Speak, Lord, for your servant hears'" (see v. 9). The Lord spoke to Samuel again. That was a turntable moment.

In this passage of Scripture, an older mentor is helping a younger person understand the clarity of God's voice. And when that voice was heard and properly deciphered, there was in it a call to action and ministry performance.

Eli had stood to the side and pushed the buttons and pulled the levers for Samuel. Because of that, the young boy is on a new track, a new level of obedience. He speaks to the people on behalf of God and becomes one of the great figures of all Scripture.

When I turned 40 I did something I try to do on every birthday. I retreated into seclusion for several hours and asked myself two questions: Where have I been this last year? and, Where am I heading?

I asked myself a few more searching questions on my fortieth birthday. Forty is a little more traumatic, you understand. So I asked: Where have I been the last 40 years? and, Should God choose, where might I go within the next 40 years?

Honestly, I was looking for some sort of vision. It didn't come.

But by the end of the day, there was one impulse that came through clearer and stronger than all the rest: The further a woman or man goes past mid-life, the more energy they need to invest into the generation that will take their place. From that point on, I decided my life should be invested in asking: Who are the young men and women I can help decode the voice of God so they can hear His call clearly?

There are periods in a young person's life that could be called turntable moments. One is the collegiate years.

The pivotal nature of those years is that students have

left one set of tracks—the influence of parents and home—but have not fully carved out or thought about their next track, one that will be defined more by such things as vocational obligations, possible marriage and a new set of friends and community responsibilities.

College years are like a parenthesis of life. Most of us, in those three to six years, begin to frame some of the most important decisions of our lives. At least that was my case. It was during those years I decided on the ministry and met my future wife, Gail.

What made all that happen for me? Six people who stood to the side of my turntable and pushed buttons and pulled levers at just the right moments. They were the Elis who helped me hear and understand God's call.

As I survey the university landscape today, some 12.3 million students, I wrestle with the question: Who's pushing the buttons and pulling the levers today to determine the direction these young people will take when they leave college?

Historically, there were a lot of people, both at home and overseas, who pushed the buttons and pulled the levers and are responsible for many generations of students hearing the call of God. Thereby, they have influenced the Student Volunteer Movement.

Years ago God gave me a hero—Charles Simeon. I've collected virtually all the literature available on his life. There are many who would argue who the real founder is of the so-called modern student movement. Yet nearly all of today's missionary effort in this area can be traced back to this one interesting, and, by the way, single man who lived in Cambridge and who was for 54 years the pastor of Cambridge University Holy Trinity Church.

Simeon was quite a believer. He was eccentric in personality, fastidious in dress, but a remarkable young man.

When he finished his student days at Cambridge, he determined to take all the procedures for ordination into the Church of England. Because his father had some clout with a few of the social structures of that country, he was able, in his own way, to push a few buttons and pull a few levers for his son. Before long, Charles Simeon was the rector of the Holy Trinity Church.

His first 14 years at Cambridge were some of the worst anyone in the ministry has ever experienced. The church congregation utterly rejected Simeon. Every Sunday morning those who owned pews made a big deal of locking them loudly when Simeon began to preach. Many times they would walk out, leaving him to preach to a near-empty church. Because the church was under the bishop's authority, the congregation couldn't push Simeon out, however.

Finally the dam broke and people began to accept this man who wouldn't go away. And the student crowd, who formerly threw rotten vegetables at Simeon, began to listen, until finally the sanctuary was jammed out. Students were hanging out windows and sitting outside the church to hear him preach.

The significance of this story is simple. Simeon was one of the first in modern times to see the genius of planting a witness in the collegiate community. Before long he began to open his home and hold conversation parties. A reproduction of his book *The Conversation Parties of the Reverend Dr. Charles Simeon,* first published in 1839, tells about the stories of Simeon's Friday evening conversation parties, when 60 or 70 students would come to his home and pelt him with questions. Scores of young men came under the receptivity of the gospel of Christ, which they may not have heard from any other source.

Later Charles Simeon got a burden for the lost nations

of the world—most particularly those in the British Empire. He began to join men like William Wilberforce, Charles Grant, Henry Thornton and John Vinn, who were all beginning to put pressure on the English government to send chaplains, hopefully missionaries, to India and other countries such as Sierra Leone. They met with heavy resistance, however.

One night in a London tavern, Simeon met with other interested parties and formed what we know today as the Church Missionary Society.

Many of the men who first went out from this society died on the field—Henry Martin, Thomas Thomason and Bishop Daniel Wilson, the first resident bishop of Calcutta. All these men were Charles Simeon products because Simeon saw the genius of working with young men in their turntable moments.

When Simeon died in 1836, thousands turned out for his funeral. Sir James Stevens said of Simeon, "If one were to know the influence that this man has had, they would realize that his influence has extended far beyond the greatest primate of England."[1]

The influence of Charles Simeon did not end with his death. He left behind a tradition of students who believe that it is not enough simply to know the gospel, one must perpetuate the good news of Jesus Christ in world evangelization.

Simeon was part of the founding of the British and Foreign Bible Society, one of the first missions organizations ministering to Jewish people on the European mainland. He was also concerned about ministering to orphans and social welfare. He purchased a factory that had been put in mothballs and opened it tho those who were unemployed. It was Simeon who started a fund, which exists today, called the Simeon Trust. This fund brought up the right in

We must be willing to push the buttons and pull the levers and inspire a whole new generation to get about the business of world evangelization."

more than 150 English parishes to appoint the resident preaching minister.

In 1827 Simeon was at the root of a group called the Jesus Lane Society. This group of Simeon followers had the vision to go out into the poorer parts of Cambridge and other communities and teach the Word of God to orphans. It was also Simeon disciples who formed the original Cambridge Union for Private Prayer in 1848. Through that tradition came the Intercollegiate Union in 1877, which for all practical purposes is the organizational grandparent of the InterVarsity movement.

While this movement was going on, there was one going on in the United States, with each emerging student generation hearing God's call under the direction of mentors, people who were pushing buttons and pulling levers.

During my time as president of InterVarsity, I came to realize the student missionary movement, if fully grasped by the Church, will reawaken its missionary zeal.

About a year ago I was in Brazil meeting with students and their mentors who carry the gospel to the universities in Rio de Janeiro, Sao Paulo and some of the major cities in the country's interior. Missions like these are run on a shoestring and are always targeted at the young people who will eventually reach to the leadership structures of their nations.

Recently I listed some of the beautiful concepts that have come out of the student movement in the last 20 years. Though not new, many have been honed in effectiveness. One example is the short-term missions concept, with thousands upon thousands of young people going out across the world. Many of these students extend their short-term commitment into the area of vocational ministry.

These short-term projects are sponsored not only by

Christian colleges and organizations such as InterVarsity and Campus Crusade, but more and more by local churches. Our former Grace Chapel congregation in Lexington, Massachusetts has averaged 70 to 100 students over the last several years who have gone out on these projects.

The kind of specialized training needed for short-term commitments, which is now available, was almost unknown 20 years ago. The new genius of language training and the whole concept of tentmaking are marvelous ways to crash through those barriers put up against the gospel.

The whole concept of international students ministering to us is also part of this modern student missionary movement.

Then there's the concept of strategic research. Again, this is not new but today it has made great strides as men and women have applied many of its tenets to the places where God is most interested in working.

These are all concepts that few people thought about 50 years ago. Or if they did, they were accused of speculating in pure fantasy. Today, however, these concepts are reality. We have the tools and the resources. Now we need the Elis and the Samuels who will help send these resources out to a lost world.

My brothers and sisters in InterVarsity and the other parachurch organizations can tell you we now face a student audience who is the next potential explosive group of missionaries. This is a group with unprecedented needs. We need prayer and support and people power like never before.

One may argue that there's always been a generation spiritually needier than the one today, but I'm not sure. We now work with a group of student recruits for the modern missions movement who are information-rich, but wisdom-poor. They know alot, but they've experienced little. This is a group rich in connections and relational networks, but poor in quality personal relationships.

Into this seemingly spiritual and psychic vacuum, there are a few people who believe in bringing in the gospel. If we can reach this group of students, I shudder to think what's possible. We could break wide open a way of bringing the gospel to the lost in a whole new way. When I look at this generation, I am reminded of Jesus getting out of His boat, looking at the crowd of 5,000 and saying, "These people are like sheep who have no shepherd" (see Matt. 9:36). That's this student generation—they're in desperate need of a shepherd.

Fifty-two percent of the students on the secular campuses today come from single-parent families. From this sort of background they bring with them all sorts of struggles—low self-esteem, resistance and resentment against authority, internal anger, a poor understanding of what leadership means, a lack of knowledge of how to make basic commitments.

This group has no role models to help them understand what a fruitful marriage is, or how one relates to children or peers. They do not understand leaders because they have had few leadership models. They don't understand how to submit to authority or give authority. And they've lost their idealism. They've retreated within themselves and ask only: How can I get ahead? How can I be secure? This is a marvelous group of young people with tremendous needs. The gospel of Jesus Christ could do so much to help capture their raw human potential and track it to a point on their turntable that could head them out in a new and exciting direction.

It's very important to realize that a large percentage of

those who went to the mission field following World War II are now heading into retirement. The attrition rate of retiring missionaries is not being covered by the numbers being sent from our shores today. This is a serious matter that we are going to reap the consequences of in a short period of time.

The possibilities of the gospel, the needs of the modern student generation are what drives me today. It's the reality of knowing that today's generation may be headed for a time when there is no frequent vision—where very few will hear the voice of God.

But it doesn't have to be that way. The world is waiting—at least the Christian world is waiting—for a few good Elis—men and women who will become partners in fostering a new student movement. The world is certainly in need, whether it knows it or not, for some good Samuels who, being mentored by the Elis, will hear and obey God's call.

In 1 Samuel, the young boy goes back to bed and again hears God's voice. This time, acting on the advice of Eli, Samuel looks up and says, "Speak, Lord. Your servant hears." And the Spirit of God whispers into the soul of young Samuel something like this: "I'm about to do something in this land that will make the ears of everybody tingle. Samuel, you will play a major role."

The next morning when Samuel awakens, Eli comes to him and says, "What have you heard?" Samuel gives the painful words, which had negative implications for Eli. But Eli, to his credit, says, "You heard God's voice, now go do it."

I'm thankful to those men and women who said to me long ago, "What you heard is God's voice. Now go do it." It's up to us to become the Elis to all the young Samuels. We must be willing to push the buttons and pull the levers and inspire a whole new generation to get about the business of world evangelization.

Note

1. Hugh Evans Hopkins, *Charles Simeon of Cambridge* (Grand Rapids, MI: Wm. B. Eerdmans, 1977).

2

World Missions 1986-2000
by
Ralph D. Winter

My contact with InterVarsity Missions began the year the Student Foreign Missions Fellowship (SFMF) tied in with InterVarsity Christian Fellowship. J. Christy Wilson, Jr., who was like a matchmaker in that marriage, recruited me to go to the first of the after-called Urbana Conferences in Toronto in 1946, which manifested and celebrated that union. When I was in college, SFMF existed but was not connected with InterVarsity. Later I helped establish an InterVarsity chapter, the first that ever existed at Caltech, my alma mater.

It isn't as if I first heard about missions at the Toronto Conference, because I grew up in a missions-minded church. But it was there that I first got the idea that you could be a tentmaker missionary. That knowledge gave me a special perspective a few months later when I read in the National Association of Evangelicals magazine that 41 American teachers of English were being sought by the government of Afghanistan. So I wrote up a rather pompous document that was then sent out all over the place, and, with Christy's cooperation, to all the 70 or so Inter-

Varsity staff. That was in the spring of 1947.

The first two to go to Afghanistan as English teachers were actually an InterVarsity couple. Several other IV staff followed later and that little trickle grew into a large group.

When my wife and I were ready to go, the one position open at the time had already been given to another couple. We had too many recruiters around! So we didn't go to the field then, but went further into graduate studies and finally ended up in Guatemala, not as tentmakers, but instead under a normal missionary board. In any case, I feel like a kissing cousin to InterVarsity and the Student Foreign Missions Fellowship.

World Missions from 1986-2000 has been the very thing over the last four years, the last four months, the last four weeks, and the last four days has been growing in profound momentum in my heart. No other single subject has ever captured my attention like this one. The year 2000 means 100 times more to me than it did earlier this year.

Let me begin with one of the final statements of Wil Norton in his history of SFMF: "It is not the future of the SFMF which is of primary concern, rather it is the future of mankind. We do not seek any earthly trophies, any institutional goals. We're part and parcel of a much larger enterprise which is the work of God in this world."

This may sound a little melodramatic, but I want to make an unusual statement: I believe we need to begin to plan in terms of the end of history.

Take a piece of paper and make a time line from 1986 to the year 2000. Then note how old you will be each year. Try to get a feel for how close we are to the year 2000. I don't mean to imply that we shouldn't have any kind of pension provision! I'm just saying, don't count too heavily on more time than the year 2000 as far as the end of history is concerned.

I'm interested in the year 1886, not so much for what led up to that time, but rather what has followed it. I'm aware of, fascinated by, and my mind and heart are fairly glued to the record of how we got where we are today. That's why I am fascinated by what Gordon MacDonald has said about what has happened in the last 20 years. Do you too sense the increasing tempo? The thing I'd like us all to be thinking and praying about is what's going to happen between now and the year 2000. That's less than 20 years away!

Let's measure our vision against that which others had a hundred years ago.

Who were those people who gathered in 1886 at the Mount Hermon Conference? What were they thinking as far as the future was concerned? We may think their thoughts were that of evangelizing the world in this generation. But that's not true. That came later. In 1886 they were thinking about evangelizing the world by the year 1900.

Now don't be embarrassed for them. That goal wasn't really an impossible task even then. It could have happened. But just because it didn't happen doesn't mean it can't happen by the year 2000. Because it didn't happen doesn't mean that Christ is never going to return.

You may have grown up as I did in a church where there was lots of prophecy talk. I used to sit there on Sunday nights in the back of the church reading the book of Revelation. I wanted to find the answers. I didn't find out a whole lot and finally gave up.

While I was studying Revelation, three of the great Bible scholars of that day—Norman Harrison, William Evans, and one whose name I can't remember—all came out with a book on Revelation. Each one had the rapture occurring at a different time and place. Some of us may be burned out on this subject; others may have little knowledge in this area. In any case, we cannot forever overlook the incessant refrain from Scripture about the end of history.

As we approach the year 2000, let's sketch some of the events that took place in the years leading up to 1886 and see if there are any parallels to those events today.

We all know about the meeting of 251 students at Mount Hermon in 1886. The site was a new school just being built for boys, about five miles downriver from the girls' school at Northfield, Massachusetts, the birthplace and focal point of Dwight L. Moody's career. That's the meeting where the famous 100 students volunteered for missions and kicked off what two years later was to be called the Student Volunteer Movement for Foreign Missions—the strongest single force for world mission impact in all of history.

Something I had not noticed until recently was a meeting that occurred a year before, in 1885, at Northfield. Three key people were at that meeting who were also present at the 1886 meeting: Dwight L. Moody, A.T. Pierson and Luther Wishard. What happened in 1885 definitely set the stage for the 1886 meeting. In fact, I believe that without the first meeting, the 1886 meeting would not have taken place. It was at the 1885 meeting that Moody was changed, Wishard was given hope and Pierson was given opportunity.

J.E.K. Studd, C.T. Studd's older brother, went on from this 1885 meeting to Cornell where, according to John R. Mott, his ministry "converted" Mott and prepared him for the 1886 meeting. This same Studd then went back to London, a key man in the development of the largest and most significant world conference on missions up until that time.

Before we go any farther, let's discuss Dwight L. Moody. The closer I get to Moody through reading some of the early documents, the more impressed I am by the man. There was no other person alive at that time who compared with him.

Moody was just an illiterate man in the eyes of many cultured people. Before he left for England, many pleaded, "Dwight, don't go to England. People there are very socially conscious. That means, you will not rate. And if you do go, don't go near the schools or universities, or you'll be laughed right off the campuses."

Moody went anyhow, and he was laughed at, but not laughed off the campuses as was predicted. He made quite an impact, not only on the people of his own social and educational level, but on many aristocrats as well.

He once had to speak at two different kinds of meetings in the same day, one right after the other. He went by fast carriage across London from Haymarket Square, which was jammed with 20,000 ordinary people, to the exclusive opera house of the aristocrats, where for streets around were carriages of the wealthy. Moody walked in as if it made any difference which auditorium he was in and poured out his heart. This "illiterate," certainly quite unsophisticated country boy was used by God to shake England to its core.

Back now to the 1885 meeting. When J.E.K. Studd attended the conference at Northfield, he hadn't yet gone to Cornell where he met John Mott. Moody had set aside a day of prayer for missions and in the evening turned things over to A.T. Pierson, who poured out his heart:

What we need is for a large meeting on the world

level representing all evangelical churches solely
to plan a worldwide campaign and to proclaim the
good tidings to every living soul in the shortest
time. Let the fields of the world be divided and distributed with as little waste of men and means as
may be. Let there be a universal appeal for workers and money and a systematic gathering of offerings that shall organize the mites into millions. [1]

At this point in Pierson's appeal, Moody, who was on
the platform, jumped to his feet, interrupted Pierson,
waved his hand to the whole 1,000 people to vote their
approval, and everybody responded. Moody wasn't often
on the subject of missions, but then and there he
appointed a committee of six, including J.E.K. Studd,
Pierson and A.J. Gordon, who later drew up a statement
called "An Appeal to Disciples Everywhere." Keep in
mind, this is the year before Mount Hermon, 1886.

The "Appeal" issued by the Northfield Convention
reads:

To fellow believers of every name scattered
throughout the world, greetings:
Assembled in the name of the Lord Jesus
Christ in one accord in one place, we have continued for ten days in prayer and supplication, com-
muning with one another about the common salvation, the blessed hope, and the duty of witnessing
to a lost world. It was near to our place of meeting
that in 1747 [You can see that these people looked
back, too. They drew from the past.] at North-
ampton, Jonathan Edwards sent forth his trumpet
appeal, calling upon disciples everywhere to unite
in prayer for a fusion of the Spirit upon the entire

habitable globe. That summons to prayer marks a new era in the history of the Church of God. Praying bands were gathered together in this and other lands. Mighty revivals of religion followed.[2]

By this date in history, immense revivals had taken place. We had the awakening of the eighteenth century. Then, towards the end of that century, a time of unprecedented secularism followed the American and French Revolutions; in the Tom Paine era there was not one student at Yale College who would admit to being a Christian. And then a mighty revival took place on that campus; the Haystack Prayer meeting convened at Williams College in 1806.

Other things happened too. For example, Charles Simeon and the great revivals of the early nineteenth century ensued. Then in 1858-59 there was a revival that shook the whole country beginning with the Fulton Street prayer meeting in New York City and reverberating clear across the continent to Portland, Oregon. There, for three months, the department stores were shut down for three hours each afternoon because there were not enough customers—everyone was praying. Now that's revival!

Now then, Satan has always wrought much evil to hold back these spiritual movements; the War Between the States broke out, and more people were killed in proportion to the population than in nearly any other war in history.

Continuing on with the "Appeal":

But the church of God is slow to move in responses to the providence of God. Nearly a thousand million of [the] human race are without the gospel. Vast districts are wholly unoccupied, so few are the laborers working.

There is an abundance of both men and means in the church to give the gospel to every living soul before this century closes [How did they figure that out? A billion people to reach.] If but 10 million out of 400 million of nominal Christians would undertake such systematic labor as that each one of that number should in the course of the 15 years [note they were looking ahead 15 years to 1900!] reach 100 other souls. Then the whole present population of the globe would have heard the good tidings by the year 1900.

We're impressed with two things which are just now of great importance. First, the immediate occupation and evangelization of every destitute district of the earth's population.[3]

Note they didn't think in terms of peoples or nations. They thought in terms of districts—geographic districts. They were talking about engaging the world, nevertheless, getting in and getting started.

Second, they spoke of a new infusion of the Spirit in answer to united prayer. What a beautiful statement of the two parts of the picture David Bryant has so skillfully blended and so wonderfully promoted in the Concerts of Prayer movement. It thrills me to hear him pronounce that 14-syllable word: "Spiritual-awakening-and-world-evangelization." It's a tremendous thought!

Pierson continues:

Therefore we earnestly appeal to all fellow disciples to join us and each other in an important daily supplication for a new and mighty infusion of the Holy Spirit upon all ministers, missionaries, evangelists, pastors, teachers and Christian workers, upon the whole earth, that God would impart to all Christ's witnesses the tongues of fire and melt hard hearts before the burning message. It is not by might of power, but by the spirit of the Lord that all true success must be secured.[4]

Now, I'm not sharing this with you to teach you anything. I'm allowing you to measure the kind of people who wrote this document.

Let us call upon God until He answers with fire. What we are to do for the salvation of the lost must be done quickly for the generation is passing away. Obedient to our marching orders, let us "go into all the world, preach the gospel to every creature" while from our very hearts we pray, "Thy Kingdom come."[5]

Of course, when they didn't make their goal by 1900, they came up with a new slogan: "Evangelization of the World in This Generation," because the generation moves along; it doesn't just stop at a certain date.

What we have just read is part of the background of the Mount Hermon Conference; I think of the SFMF movement as the background for 1986. But I think it's erroneous, unfair and illegitimate—however scholarly—to try to make comparisons between the SVM movement and the SFMF movement. The SVM was able to build upon this movement about which we have just read. By contrast, SFMF was born in the middle of the Depression, and had many strikes against it.

Only today have we arrived where those 1886 students were back then. In 1936 the SFMF was having to start over again.

Sometimes we read about the buildup of the SVM almost like it started in a vacuum. On the contrary, there were many streams that made it possible, streams that were not present in 1936.

For example, I hope to see a dissertation on the carryover between the Christian Endeavor movement and the SVM. By the year 1886, there were 16,000 of these young people's groups on church campuses all across this country. And in every local Christian Endeavor fellowship there was always a missionary committee with a strong missionary message.

Christian Endeavor was already a national movement and would shortly be international, long before the Student Volunteer Movement. In 1892 totally independent of SVM, Christian Endeavor had 30,000 young people at a meeting in Madison Square Garden. The only connection to the SVM was that Robert E. Speer, one of the SVM leaders, was asked to be a speaker.

There was another mighty stream of power that was an immense reality: the women's mission movement. Ironically, the missionary movement in this country was the remarkable oddity that allowed the birth of the feminist movement. Most of the elite women's colleges in this country were born and achieved real headway because of the women's missionary movement, which allowed and suggested that women go to college in order to be missionaries. The college catalogs at Wellesley, Radcliffe and Mount Holyoke don't say anything about this interesting fact, however. By 1886 there were something like 56,000 women's missionary fellowships throughout this country.

Another factor in the meteoric rise of the SVM was the institutional miracle for the highly evangelical YMCA of that day. SFMF in 1936 had no way to hitch its wagon to that kind of star. When John R. Mott entered the YMCA circuit in 1887, as the traveling secretary, he married Luther Wishard's sister from Oberlin College. Then he got on a Pullman train for a 5,000-mile honeymoon trip to the West Coast. He went all the way to, and up and down, the Coast and home again without paying a single cent; the railroad industry gave him the tickets.

Now the railroad leaders weren't that interested in missions. It was just that by 1886 the YMCA was a financially impressive enterprise. Unlike J. Christy Wilson, Jr., who didn't even know how he could get money for a car or where to have an office or who was going to pay his salary when he joined InterVarsity as the missions director in 1946, when Mott became secretary, he stepped into a gilded carriage. He traveled first-class from that day on for the next 32 years, because he was working within that immense financial empire of lay people with money.

It would be as if the SFMF were getting financial backing from the Full Gospel Businessmen's Association International! On that trip, all Mott had to do was send a cable saying he needed $25,000, which in those days was like $250,000, to build a new YMCA in such and such a town, and whoosh, the money would be there.

When Mott went to Southern California, there were already eight colleges in that wild-west frontier. And when he got off the train, he was invited to a meeting sponsored by the local YMCA collegiate groups. Faculty from all eight colleges came to hear this unknown man of 25 who had only been married a few days. Six of the college presidents even turned out. Now this was not due to the strategic maneuvering of those young leaders. It was simply that they walked into a powerful machine that became a carrier vehicle for the SVM movement.

What we need to be looking at and comparing is what, by 1886, God was preparing them to do by the year 1900, and what, by 1986, He is preparing us to do by the year 2000."

There is one other factor. And that is, the whole country was wide awake to world conquest. Now, surely Americans weren't interested in world conquest, were they? And certainly we didn't have any colonial empire in mind. Or did we? Listen! In those days Americans were thirsting for world conquest. Now I don't recommend this as a helpful backdrop for missionary expansion; I only note it as one of the factors in the reality of the social world back then.

It was during the next two years after Mount Hermon, before the SVM was officially organized, that we admitted six new states to the Union—six states right along the Canadian border. We wanted to keep those Canadians out of the Northwest Territory. We were chauvinists in that sense, determined to get the land. We moved south and took over Cuba, then Puerto Rico, and across the Pacific and took over the Philippine Islands, Guam and half of the Samoan Islands. We were ready to conquer the world.

About this time a group of Methodist ministers met with President McKinley. He told them he had been praying the night before about what to do with the Philippine Islands, and he said, "God told me that we needed to get in there and take hold of things and lift people up in the name of Christ."

Now I'm not recommending that kind of political philosophy, but rather am noting that the Student Volunteer Movement had this kind of a mighty secular wind behind it. In this case, Christians were encouraged to think in terms of going into the whole world. The SFMF in 1936 did not have this kind of international mood behind it! That's why it's unfair to say, "What went wrong with the SFMF that it didn't boom into existence? Didn't they pray enough?"

What we need to be looking at and comparing is what, by 1886, God was preparing them to do by the year 1900, and what, by 1986, He is preparing us to do by the year 2000.

The Student Foreign Missions Fellowship has done a tremendous job. The impact they have had on missions has been greater through the secular campuses, which it has affected through the Urbana conventions, than through its work on the Christian school campuses. One reason for this is because of the massive shift of evangelical students to secular campuses. Ninety percent of all the children of evangelical families in this country will never even step foot on a Christian college campus.

Let me just add a few dabs of paint to the picture of the last 20 years, from my own experience. More than any other factor, it was Urbana, sponsored by InterVarsity, that rocked me out of my job as professor at Fuller Seminary. There I was, concentrating on the field situation, but watching all the while what was going on at Urbana. Historically, the attendance at the Urbana meetings has always gone steadily up. But the percentage of students signing the cards was gradually going down, until the bottom was hit in 1970, when only 7 percent signed.

Of course, that was following the '60s when satanic powers came against God's Church. But somehow the gospel and the power of salvation boiled up through all that harassment and confusion, and by 1973, a perceptible shift had taken place. Suddenly, the difficult-to-measure change of mood became concretely recorded when the 7 percent Urbana decision makers became 28 percent, then 60 percent, then 70 percent and so on. The last few times the percentage signed at Urbana has been so high that nobody counts anymore. A major change has taken place that cannot be registered merely in terms of attendance. We now measure in terms of commitment, and it's phenomenal!

I proposed to David Howard, who was then in charge

of Urbana, that we call upon mission leaders to help set up
a special missions training program for students, to help
them make their shift from Urbana to a platform of solid
facts upon which to decide their futures. I also suggested,
for the students' sake, the course carry college credits.

Today we have a 900-page reader and study guide, and
this year we have 63 locations around the country where
the four-semester-unit course is taught. We're grinding
out about 1,500 students a year; at least 1,200 alumni are
already on the mission field. Most of these students have
resulted from the interfacing of InterVarsity with other
campus groups. It doesn't belong to any one organization
any longer. It's God's ball game.

We can't even properly answer all the letters that
come to us from campuses and churches all across the
country. A church in Escondido writes: "We're not a campus, but couldn't we offer this course in our church?"

We replied, "Hey, church people aren't up to a course
that requires 200 hours in 15 weeks!"

They came back with, "We would like to do it."

So they got 21 churches who sent a total of 121 students. Now three other churches in the same area are
doing the same thing. One retired couple taking the course
decided to sell their beautiful home and move into a trailer.
George Miley, who was running the program, was for 18
years in charge of two Operation Mobilization ships. When
he heard what the couple wanted to do, he went over and
pleaded with them not to sell their house.

"We're going to get a bad name if we have that kind of
influence around here," George counseled.

But the couple couldn't be changed, and the wife
answered, "George, if we don't do this, we feel we'll be
condemned to mediocrity."

This kind of response indicates that there is a new

mood, a new seriousness about missions. So many things are happening all over the country that reflect this new interest.

There are students traveling around in vans, trying to mobilize other students to become missionaries. The Caleb Project met 13,000 students this way in the fall of 1985. They've now connected up with a number of mission agencies and this year expect to travel in four separate vans and meet 30,000 students face-to-face.

Recently I discovered something interesting. I was preparing a paper for the annual meeting of the American Society of Church History and had drawn up a chart of the attendance at the Student Volunteer Missions quadrennials. Their peak was in Des Moines with 6,000 students. Now if you divide that number by the student population in those days, it would be six times the highest attendance of Urbana. Thus, although the student population in those days was paltry, for 6,000 of them to show up at an SVM convention was quite something! Even our Urbana conventions are a minor ripple by comparison. In those days the Student Volunteers shook the entire college world. Urbana is not doing that.

But we must not make comparisons and say we have failed. We need to consider these Urbana conventions as a marvelous rebuilding of the foundations of a new and bigger mission movement than the world has ever seen. They are only a runner-up to a future that will be unbelievably exciting.

When those collegians were meeting in Northfield in 1886 and talking about winning the world for Christ by 1900, it was already true in the state of Massachusetts that 68 of the major towns and cities were ruled by Catholics who had recently moved in. Massachusetts was already slipping out of the hands of the evangelical tradition. The year of the Statue of Liberty was 1886 and all around this country there was a tremendous influx of immigration. Those immigrants weren't evangelicals, and I'm sure they were resented by a lot of people. What's more, this massive new influx bogged down the entire country. No longer did we have any kind of national Protestant consensus.

But things have changed since then. The children of those Europeans have grown up in our communities. Many of them have become members of evangelical churches, so that the evangelical movement today is literally stronger than it was back then. America has gone through a long period of assimilating all those new people.

My theme is "1986 and the year 2000." Let's take a look at just what it would take to finish the task. In 1986 and 1987 we must reach out to 1,000 new people groups, another 2,000 in 1988 and 2,000 every year after that until by 1995 every one of these remaining groups will have been reached. If it were even remotely possible back in 1886 to finish evangelizing the world by 1900, it is eminently feasible today to complete it by the year 2000.

The total population figures of the world today are much larger than they were 100 years ago, but the gain of the evangelical proportion is extremely significant. I'm referring to the explosive growth of the vital forces—the evangelical believers and churches and mission societies that are springing up all over the world.

How many mission fields are there today? Let's say there are 17,000 unreached people's groups. How many evangelical congregations are there in the world today? Would you believe two and one-half million? That means there are 150 times as many congregations as there are groups to be reached, or to put it another way, there are 150 congregations per group.

If only one out of every 10 of those 150 churches would wake up to the reality of evangelization potential we could readily, with only one-tenth of those churches, penetrate every group by the year 1995. Then, in 1995, we would have to engage each remaining group. We need to allow the five years between 1995 and 2000 to make sure that the ripples of the gospel get to every human being within every group.

Will we fall short in completing the task, as we did 100 years ago? If that new infusion of the Spirit—those fires of revival—don't sweep this country, and if the evangelical population of America today is paralyzed by affluence and all kinds of concerns, then we may fall short again!

Christ reigns. Are we with Him? Are we going to go with Him where He wants to go? Or are we just going to commemorate people who had something that we don't have?

Notes

1. John Pollack, *Moody—The Biography* (Chicago: Moody, 1983), p. 277.
2. A.T. Pierson, *Crises in Missions* (Publisher unknown, 1886).
3. Ibid.
4. Pollack, *Moody.*
5. Ibid.

3

What Can We Learn from the Student Volunteer Movement?

by
J. Christy Wilson, Jr.

In the early part of this century, there was a student who was seeking God's will for his life. He put a map of the world above his bed and would kneel beside it and pray, "Lord, if you spare me and if you tarry, I will be serving you somewhere in this world. I am willing to go wherever you lead. Show me where you want me to go."

As the student studied the needs of the world, he felt God calling him to Iran along the border of Afghanistan. He eventually went there in 1919 and served faithfully as an evangelistic missionary for 43 years. This student volunteer was Dr. William Miller who now lives in Philadelphia and is 94 years old.

Before he went to the mission field and while he was still studying, he had prayer meetings in his room every noon. He invited other students to intercede with him for laborers—as Jesus said, "Pray . . . the Lord of the harvest, that he will send forth labourers into his harvest" (Matt. 9:38, *KJV*). They took that command and promise of Christ seriously.

Dr. Miller then became a traveling secretary visiting schools to recruit volunteers. And before he went to Mashad, in eastern Iran, he got over 100 students to give their lives for foreign missions. One of these was Dr. Philip Howard, the father of David Howard, who headed up two Urbana student missionary conventions and is now the director of the World Evangelical Fellowship. Another was Elisabeth Elliot, whose husband was martyred by the Auca Indians. Dr. Philip Howard went with the Belgian Gospel Mission.

Dr. Miller also got my parents to sign the Student Volunteer Movement card. My father had just finished seminary and was headed as a chaplain with the American army in Europe. He was to sail from New York City on November 12, 1918. But on November 11, Armistice was declared. My father was very disappointed, not that the war was over, but that he had said good-bye to all his friends, and they had had commissioning services for him before going overseas.

Bill Miller came to call on him and said, "Christy, you have been so anxious to go overseas for your country, how about going overseas for your Lord?" My father accepted the challenge. In 1919 he and my mother, along with Bill Miller, sailed for Iran.

My grandfather could not understand why my father had gone to the mission field. He thought the reason was that he couldn't get a church in the States. And he kept writing, "I'm sure there must be a church somewhere that would be willing to have you as pastor." Yet my parents spent 20 exciting years as missionaries in Iran, as a result of the Student Volunteer Movement.

Many have called the SVM the greatest student missionary movement in history. Dr. James McCosh, former president of Princeton University, wrote about it: "Never in any age has there been a presentation of living men and women to compare to this, except in the time of Pentecost."[1] But what's happened to the Student Volunteer Movement? What can we learn from it?

The Intercession for Laborers

First of all, we can learn the importance of intercession. The Student Volunteer Movement was born in prayer. Its antecedent was the Haystack Prayer Meeting in Williams College in 1806. There the first foreign missionary movement started in the United States as five students met to pray. They not only interceded for unreached people, they dedicated their lives to missions saying, "We can do it if we will."

Later, Luther Wishart who was a student at Princeton University with Woodrow Wilson visited the haystack monument in 1879. On top of this marble memorial is a globe of the world. Some students, apparently as a prank, have twisted it so the poles are at an angle. This can illustrate the fact that through prayer the world can be turned upside down. On the front of the monument is a bas-relief of the haystack and the words of Christ, "The field is the world." Then below are inscribed the names of the five students who prayed there. Luther Wishart knelt in the snow in front of it and prayed, "Lord, do it again." And God did it again.

In the summer of 1885, Dwight L. Moody held a conference at Northfield, Massachusetts with over 1,000 in attendance. There a call was issued to all Christians to evangelize the world before the end of that century. Wishart, who was also there as a traveling secretary for the Intercollegiate YMCA, sent to Moody and asked if he would call a conference the next summer for students. So 251 students came to Mount Hermon in 1886. This was to be the answer to Luther Wishart's prayer for God to do it again.

Robert Wilder, who was an undergraduate at Princeton University, and his older sister Grace, who had graduated from Mount Holyoke in 1883, prayed for a year that God would call a hundred of those students who were coming to that conference to sign the card to become missionaries to unevangelized portions of the world. And that's what happened. That prayer was literally fulfilled.

Wilder attended the conference for male leaders of the Intercollegiate YMCA, which lasted from July 7 to August 2, 1886. It was not planned to be a missionary conference, but was to be a time when they would learn to use the Bible and music in evangelism. The Holy Spirit, however, worked in a mighty way and altered the emphasis to focus on the evangelization of the world.

Wilder got 21 students who already were planning to go to the mission field to sign a pledge. Then they prayed for the other students. With only eight days remaining, Moody allowed missionary meetings to be held. By the end of the conference there were 99 students who had signed the pledge that they were desirous and willing, God permitting, to become foreign missionaries. And at the final meeting as these volunteers were on their knees praying, the one-hundredth student came and knelt with them and asked for a card. Why? Because of prayer.

Grace and Robert Wilder then prayed for 1,000 more to sign and pledge the next year. But God did exceedingly abundantly above what they asked, because 2,106 others volunteered during the 1886-87 academic year.

The Student Foreign Missions Fellowship also started with prayer. At Ben Lippen in 1936, students and leaders held whole days of prayer, seeking God. Also before the SFMF-IVCF Toronto Convention in 1946, Stacey Woods, the general secretary of InterVarsity, said that he had never seen as much prayer offered for any conference. That was the reason God worked. Of the 575 students who attended, over half went to the mission field. One of those students was Jim Elliot, another was David Howard and another was Ralph Winter. In answer to intercession God does the impossible in relation to the evangelization of the world. The power of prayer for laborers is one thing we can learn from the Student Volunteer Movement.

The Visitation of God's Holy Spirit

Dwight L. Moody was the most successful evangelist in Chicago. But there were two women who would sit in the front row of the tabernacle. They shocked him by saying, "Mr. Moody, we are praying that you will be filled with the Holy Spirit." Hearing them say this made him angry. He thought, "Why don't they go and pray for others who are not as successful as I am."

Later he tells about going down a street in New York City when the Holy Spirit came on him with such power that he had to ask God to stop; he was afraid he was going to be killed. He went to a friend's home and asked if he could be alone. He went up to the bedroom, shut the door and spent hours alone with the Lord. After that, Moody was used not only in Chicago but throughout North America and the British Isles as well.

Moody never could speak English correctly. Until his dying day he used expressions like "he don't" and "she don't." Dr. Charles Spurgeon said that Moody was the only man he had heard who could pronounce Mesopotamia in one syllable.

When Moody was speaking at Cambridge University, all the students would pound their feet on the floor every

The early leaders of the Student Volunteer Movement were filled with and guided by the Spirit of God."

time he made a grammatical error. But he kept right on with his message. Following one service a student came forward and said, "Mr. Moody, I jotted down every grammatical error you made on this sheet of paper and I want to give it to you so that it will help you with your English."

Moody looked at the student and said, "I know that I make grammatical errors. But I'm using all the grammar I know for the glory of God. Are you using all the grammar you know for the glory of God?"

The next morning a leader of the student body came to him and said, "Mr. Moody, I have come to apologize. We English people pride ourselves in being gentlemen, but last night we were all very rude and you were the gentleman." Moody then led him to Christ. This broke the dam of ridicule and opposition, and more students at Cambridge came to the Lord through that mission than anytime in the history of that university. This also resulted in the missionary team of the Cambridge Seven, who as outstanding students dedicated their lives to go to China with Dr. Hudson Taylor.[2]

After an all-night prayer meeting in Ireland, Moody heard someone say, "The world has yet to see what God can do through one person who is completely yielded in His hand." Moody said, "By the help of the Holy Spirit, I want to be that person." Even though he had the handicap of a lack of education, God used him mightily, because Moody was completely dedicated. The early leaders of the Student Volunteer Movement were filled with and guided by the Spirit of God.

Robert Wilder attended a gathering held at Hartford, Connecticut in 1883. There he heard and met Dr. A.J. Gordon who had just been filled with the Holy Spirit at Moody's Northfield Conference.

Wilder wrote, "The address which most moved the

delegates was one by Dr. Adoniram Judson Gordon of Boston. He said that he had been in the ministry 20 years before he yielded himself fully to the inspiration and control of the Holy Spirit. He confessed that during those 20 years, his preaching was like using a bow and arrow where the results depended entirely on the strength of the archer. Since he had yielded himself to the influence of the Holy Spirit, he testified that the effort of his preaching had been more like the effort of using a rifle and pulling the trigger. I asked Dr. Gordon whether I must wait 20 years before laying aside my bow and arrow and taking up the rifle? With his wonderful smile he replied, 'God is ready to give you the power of His Holy Spirit as soon as you are ready to obey him.'"[3] And Robert Wilder was filled with the Holy Spirit. He said the greatest Bible study he had ever experienced was to go through the Scriptures from Genesis to Revelation studying the Person and work of the Holy Spirit.

The Evangelization of Individuals

Dwight L. Moody took to heart Psalm 96:2, which states, "Show forth his salvation from day to day" (ASV). For much of his life, Moody made it a habit to speak to at least one non-Christian about his or her soul every day. One time he went to bed, and thinking back over the day he realized he had not witnessed to a non-Christian. So he got up, dressed and went out. He found a man under a streetlight and asked him, "Are you saved?"

The man answered, "It's none of your business."

Moody replied, "It's the only business I've got." He then went back to bed and felt he had been too brash.

Later on the man came to him and said, "Ever since you spoke to me I have been miserable. What you said went like an arrow to my heart. No, I haven't been saved.

Please help me." And Moody led him to find peace in Christ.

Many came to Christ through the Student Volunteer Movement. Robert Wilder would get Christian students at Princeton University to pray for an unbelieving student for a week. Then when they talked to the student, he was usually ready to accept the Lord. When the Urbana student missionary conventions were started, they were not planned as a means to lead people to Christ. But in every one of them, many have come to the Lord.

For example, a student was interested in a girl and found out she was going to an Urbana convention. He had never heard of it and asked her what it was. She said it was a conference on vocational planning. So he went with her to Urbana in 1973. When Bily Graham gave the invitation for salvation, he accepted Christ as his Savior. Since then, he has gone through seminary, served on the foreign field and is now working in this country with international students.

The Devotion of Lives to Missions

Grace and Robert Wilder not only recruited many for the mission field, they went abroad themselves. Grace was instrumental in getting 34 women students at Mount Holyoke College to sign pledges to become foreign missionaries. She then sailed for India in 1887. Robert Wilder, after recruiting several thousand for the mission field, also went to India and had years of fruitful service there, mainly with students.

Dr. Gordon MacDonald has stated that the great need in campuses today is for dedicated leaders. And that is what happens when Christians pray. God raises up shepherds for His sheep. Leaders are needed who not only will recruit others but also will devote their lives for missions.

Improvisation with Ingenuity and Creativity

Moody did not hesitate to break norms in order to get God's work done. At one of his evangelistic meetings in London, a pastor was asked to give a short invocation. He began praying all around the world. A young doctor who had been making calls on patients came by the meeting and thought he would drop in to see what was happening. As he heard the pastor's long-winded supplications, he got up to leave. Moody kept his eyes open during the prayer. He held that Scripture did not say that he had to close them.

When he saw this young man walking out, he jumped up and said, "While our brother finishes his prayer, let's sing a hymn." As he announced the song, this young doctor turned around and thought, "There is a person who is down to earth. I'd like to hear what he has to say." He stayed, was converted and gave his life to be a missionary. That was Dr. Wilfred Grenfell, who later established a mission in Labrador.

Someone once came to Moody and asked, "Is it all right for Christians to use tainted money?" Moody answered, "The only taint about tainted money is that it t'aint enough. You give me tainted money and I'll show you how to use it for God's glory." People loved coming to Moody's meeting because they never knew what was going to happen.

At a missionary meeting held on the Northfield campus during the summer of 1885, Dr. A.T. Pierson challenged the audience to plan a worldwide campaign to proclaim the good tidings to every living soul in the shortest possible time. Moody jumped to his feet, interrupted the message and proposed that they immediately set up a committee of seven, including himself, to draw up a proposal to evangelize the world before the end of the century. A few days later they issued "An Appeal to Disciples Everywhere." It stated that with the whole world accessible there should be an immediate occupation and evangelization of every district. It also called for prayer for a new effusion of the Holy Spirit to accomplish this.

Declaration of Missionary Commitment

The Student Volunteer Movement had a pledge and those who signed it dedicated their lives to missions. The SFMF and InterVarsity also have decision cards to sign. Robert Wilder came to Hope College when Samuel Zwemer was a senior. Wilder displayed a map of India, and in front of it he had a metronome going back and forth. He stated that every time it clicked, someone died in India who had never heard the gospel. When Samuel Zwemer heard that, he determined as soon as Robert Wilder finished speaking to go forward and sign the Student Volunteer Movement card. After he made this decision, he went to the Islamic world and became perhaps the greatest missionary in history to the Muslims. Over 100,000 signed the SVM decision card of whom more than 20,500 actually went to mission fields around the world.

Consecration Even unto Death

The Student Volunteers demonstrated consecration; they were ready to sacrifice for their Lord. Dr. Zwemer wanted to go to the people in the hardest mission field in the world. After study, he determined this would be to the Muslims of Arabia. But no mission agency would send him.

He said, "If a mission board won't send you, and God calls you, bore a hole through the board and go anyway." He got another young man, a Dr. Cantine to go with him.

They went to different churches and each raised the other's support. Then they started the Arabia Mission and traveled first to Beirut, then to Cairo, after which they sailed all around the Arabian peninsula.

The two finally located mission stations in Busra, Bahrain, Kuwait and Muscat. Since this is one of the hottest areas in the world, they suffered from the temperatures. One young man who was an ordained pastor joined them, but lived only a few months, dying of heat prostration. Peter Zwemer, Samuel's younger brother, succumbed to disease after only a few years of service.

A missionary nurse who was headed for Baghdad arrived from Australia. Her mission board asked Samuel Zwemer to meet and assist her on her journey. When the two met they fell in love. But she had signed an agreement that if she resigned from the mission before her term of service was up, she would pay for her passage out. So before they could marry, he had to refund her transportation.

God gave the Zwemers children on the island of Bahrain. But two of their little girls died in one week. The Muslims at first refused to give permission for them to be buried there since they said as Christians they would contaminate the soil. Finally they allowed the burial if Dr. Zwemer would dig the graves himself. He dug two little graves, put up headstones and wrote on them the words, "Worthy is the Lamb who was slain to receive riches."

One mission sent 70 workers to Cameroon in Africa; 68 died there. Missionaries' average lifetime after they arrived was only a year and a half. Many of them took their coffins along, knowing the chances were small of returning alive. An African Christian said, "Even though the early missionaries made mistakes, they loved us and gave their lives for us."

The True Liberation of Women

Liberation of women was experienced as they became involved in missions. The first year of the Student Volunteer Movement, over 500 women signed the card that they were desirous and willing to become foreign missionaries. By the time of the second world war, women outnumbered men in Protestant missions two to one.

Corrie tenBoom, after getting out of the German concentration camp, traveled around the world to visit and witness to prisoners in many countries. She had a special ministry to them since she had been imprisoned herself. In the process she also visited many missions and was amazed to find that Protestant women outnumbered the men. Her comment was, "I am sure that when the Lord called different men to go, they answered, 'Here am I, send my sister.'"

God used women in a mighty way through the Student Volunteer Movement. They established many missionary societies in churches, organized mission agencies and sent women as doctors, evangelists and teachers all over the world. Most of these women's organizations have been merged with other groups and have lost their missionary vision. A great need today is to revive the women's missionary societies in local congregations as well as their sending agencies.

The Organization of the Movement

God used the organizational structure of the Student Volunteer Movement for foreign missions to increase and sustain its effectiveness. Officially set up in 1888, SVM bands were established in schools across the country to get those who had signed the pledge together for prayer, study and mutual encouragement. The first SVM convention was held in Cleveland in 1891. These later became the

SVM quadrennials, which were held in different locations every four years enabling every generation of students to attend one conference during their college course. The first Toronto Student Missionary Convention was patterned after these, and the Urbana gatherings have continued this model.

The Visualization of Mission Facts

The early student volunteers used maps with the words: "The Evangelization of the World in This Generation." They also had posters illustrating the unevangelized with black squares for every 1 million people from the Hindu, Buddhist and animist blocks. They had green squares for the millions of unreached Muslims. Students would put these posters up in their rooms in order to pray for the unevangelized people's groups around the world. So the SVM used early media methods and visuals even as Inter-Varsity shows Twentyonehundred Productions at Urbana and in various college chapters across Canada and the U.S.

The Publication of Mission Materials

The Student Volunteer Movement established a press to put out books and mission materials. In like manner Nav-Press, Campus Crusade for Christ and InterVarsity Press have also printed missionary publications.

When Dr. and Mrs. Ralph Winter went to the mission field in Guatemala with a denominational board, they discovered they were getting approximately twice as much salary as most of the faith missionaries. They decided they could live on the same amount as the others. Therefore, they returned half of their salary to their mission agency. But their board had the policy of paying the missionaries around the world the same salary, based on the cost of living differential published weekly from Washington, D.C. If they had accepted this return of half the salary, it would have spoiled their system. So they sent the money back to the Winters, who then decided they would still live on half their salary and deposited the rest in a savings account. With that money they were able to start the William Carey Library that has subsequently published and distributed millions of copies of mission books.

Mission Education Through Study Groups
In 1914 there were over 40,000 students in mission classes in more than 700 colleges, universities and Bible schools across the United States and Canada. Dr. John R. Mott said, "Facts are the fuel that fires missionary passion." Thus not only those who went abroad but those who stayed at home had a vision for missions. This resulted in enlightened prayer interest and financial support.

The Cooperation with Other Groups
The SVM worked with churches, mission boards and schools. Many educational institutions raised support to send their own graduates as missionaries. Money was sacrificially pledged by students who didn't have much. The volunteers however were associated with mission boards and had home churches. Many also were supported by congregations and went to fields around the world through missionary agencies.

Personalization of Support
There was also personalization in giving for individuals in missions. Contributions usually would not go into a general fund but were designated for specific persons. Different ones who went out from various schools had student

bodies praying for them and giving toward their support. When they returned from the field, they would increase interest in missions and challenge others to service abroad.

Itineration for Recruitment

At the beginning of the SVM, Robert Wilder and John Forman took a year off from their schooling to travel to educational institutions in North America to recruit volunteers. They visited 162 schools in one year and were able to get 2,106 to sign the card that stated, "I am desirous and willing, if God permits, to be a foreign missionary."

There were also Student Foreign Missions Fellowship teams that went out and enlisted many to sign their volunteer card. In similar manner there are vans of students now going to campuses around the country with the Caleb Project recruiting students for missions. If the various student organizations cooperate in missions, this can result in the greatest missionary movement in history among youth.

Dedication of Outstanding Leaders

Robert E. Speer wanted to study law with the goal of becoming Chief Justice of the U.S. Supreme Court. It is said that he along with Aaron Burr were the brightest students ever to be at Princeton University. Robert Wilder challenged Speer to give his life to missions and Speer signed the SVM pledge. While he was studying in seminary, he was called to be the head of the Board of Foreign Missions of the Presbyterian Church. This agency then had approximately 150 missionaries. Speer served as executive secretary for 46 years, at the end of which time he had built up the number of missionaries on the field to 1750, an increase of over 1000 percent.

Evangelization of the World as the Goal

Dr. A.T. Pierson, at the first conference in Mount Hermon, said, "All should go and go to all." And he is the one credited with the origin of the motto of the SVM: The Evangelization of the World in our Generation. He pointed out that every generation has this responsibility because of the clear command of Christ. This is God's goal for Christians today as well.

Conviction of an Infallible Bible

There was trust in the infallibility of the Scriptures. The early Student Volunteers believed in the full trustworthiness of the revelation and inspiration of the Word of God. But higher criticism and liberalism came like a flood into the movement. One reason for this was that officers who came into the SVM were representational of member organizations and churches rather than those who subscribed to an evangelical confessional basis of faith.

Dr. Kenneth Scott Latourette, the great scholar of mission history, had his faith shaken. He had gone as a missionary to China, but his health broke and he had to return to the United States. He later became an agnostic. Latourette took time off to go camping in the Northwest where in the midst of God's creation he regained his faith in the Lord and in His Word. He recounts this experience in his autobiography, *Beyond the Ranges*.[4] He later became professor of missions at Yale University.

By the time of the 1921 SVM Quadrennial, the liberal leadership had taken over. They claimed the older leaders like Robert Wilder, John R. Mott and Robert E. Speer were not in touch with the thinking of the student world of that day. From then on the SVM went downhill. Finally in 1969 they voted themselves out of existence. Since they (the new SVM leadership) no longer believed the Bible, there was no need to bother about missions. That is the reason God raised up the SFMF and InterVarsity, whose officers accepted the authority of the Scriptures by subscribing to a basis of faith and thus took seriously the mandate of the evangelization of the world. This has also been true of other evangelical student movements like the Navigators, Youth for Christ and Campus Crusade.

Diversification of Organizations
Many organizations trace their origin to the Student Volunteer Movement. The World Student Christian Federation, the International Missionary Council and eventually the World Council of Churches owe their beginnings to the SVM. A similar diversification of ministries for example has come from the Youth for Christ movement, which has resulted in the Billy Graham Evangelistic Association, World Vision, the Greater Europe Mission and the Lausanne Committee for the World Evangelization and other Christian organizations. Also, InterVarsity has expanded into the International Fellowship of Evangelical Students, and Campus Crusade has spawned many ministries.

Alteration of the Definition of Terms
With the liberalization of the Student Volunteer Movement, there was also an alteration of terms and their definitions. To begin with, students were challenged to go to "the unevangelized portions of the world." Later this was changed to a call to become "a foreign missionary." The goal was then altered to "Christians missions." Later this was changed to "mission." Bishop Stephen Neill said, "If 'mission' means everything, it means nothing."

The term *ecumenics* was also substituted for "missions." Dr. Samuel Zwemer, who spoke at the first SFMF/

IVCF Missionary Convention held at Toronto in 1946, said that Satan on the mount of temptation gave Jesus an ecumenical view of the world and offered it to Him if He would bow down and worship him. But Jesus rejected that and went to another mount called Calvary where He died for the sins of the world. He then appeared to His disciples on another mount called Olivet where He gave the Great Commission to go into all the world and preach the gospel to every creature. Dr. Zwemer said in *ecumenics* you lift up your eyes and look, but in *missions* you lift up your feet and go.

The term *missionary* was also changed to "fraternal worker" to emphasize the importance of the place of national Christians, who were the result of missions. But this overlooked the need for cross-cultural missionaries from all continents to reach unreached people groups, who number about half the population of the world.

Glorification of God through Such Movements

In John 12:28 Jesus prays, "Father, glorify Thy name." And the answer came from heaven, "I have both glorified it, and will glorify it again" *(NASB)*. God has glorified His name through organizations like the Student Volunteer Movement, the Student Foreign Missions Fellowship, the InterVarsity Christian Fellowship, Youth for Christ, the Navigators, Campus Crusade for Christ and others. But the work of these groups has only been preparatory to what is needed to accomplish the evangelization of the world. Christ promised that all the peoples of the earth are going to be reached when He said, "This gospel of the kingdom shall be preached in the whole world for a witness to all nations [or peoples groups], and then the end shall come" (Matt. 24:14, *NASB*).

But the question is, What part are you going to play in the evangelization of Christ's world for which He died and rose again and to which He is coming back to rule? The only answer is to be dedicated to prayer and involved in a universal revival that will result in the *evangelization of the world in our generation.*

Notes

1. Robert Wilder, *The SVM—Its Origin and Early Years* (New York: SVM, 1935) p. 22.
2. The Cambridge Seven consisted of Montagu H.P. Beauchamp, William W. Cassels, Dixon Edward Hoste, Authur Polhill-Turner, Cecil Polhill-Turner, Stanley P. Smith and Charles Thomas "C.T." Studd. For awhile after graduation from Cambridge (1883-84) these seven men traveled the British Isles, sharing their vision and burden for China with all who would listen. In February, 1885 they sailed for China, followed in years to come by scores of other students influenced by these men.
3. Wilder, *The SVM—Its Origin and Early Years*, p. 8.
4. Kenneth Scott Latourette, *Beyond the Ranges: An Autobiography* (Grand Rapids, MI: Wm. B. Eerdmans, 1962).

4

Pioneering in World Missions: Looking Back and Looking Forward

by
Elizabeth Cridland

I was reading in Job 32 recently about Elihu in which he said, "I'm the youngest, so I didn't speak right away because I gave way to age and wisdom." So I take it that Elihu's qualifications for a speaker were age and wisdom. I have just one of those, but he left out one other that I do have. And that is steps ordered by the Lord. Young people, there is nothing to begin to compare with letting the Lord order your steps.

I learned a new word in the last two or three weeks from a telecast message—*serendipity*. You probably know the word from your college training, but somehow I never came across it; it wasn't part of my vocabulary. But it is now. I'll give you my definition of the word: an unexpected, unsought for, undeserved pleasure or surprise.

Oh, how many serendipities there have been in letting the Lord order my steps. As I represent those who are seeking to look back in pioneering of world missions and then a bit forward, I just thank the Lord for all those wonderful joys and surprises He's brought into my life. Among those wonderful serendipities are the people who have crossed my path and who have had an impact on my life.

To them I pay tribute and for them I give thanks. They are the ones who helped mold and make me into what the Lord is wanting for His glory.

As we look back on missions, I like to refer to Bible characters and what they say to us modern-day missionaries. And this time it's a new character for me. I got acquainted with him all over again—the apostle Peter. And I thought, wouldn't it have been wonderful to see him coming out of that prayer meeting into the outer court area of the Temple to be the spokesman for all those first pioneers of the new era? He stood there boldly proclaiming the resurrection of the Lord Jesus Christ. He was showing forth the appropriation of that power that Paul prayed for all of us: That we might know that power by which God raised the Lord Jesus from the dead, power which we must appropriate to live the new life we find in Him (see Phil. 3:10).

Now on to the Student Volunteer Movement and the Student Foreign Missions Fellowship and all those who have experienced resurrection power in the work of world missions. May I make our look backward personal? It begins at America's Keswick when conference leaders called Dr. Robert McQuilkin back from Columbia, South Carolina, where he had gone to start Columbia Bible College. Now I had grown up in a church where I had never had a Bible opened in the church school that we in my family intermittently attended. But I went to the Keswick conference at the invitation of two dear friends and learned so many wonderful things all in one week, first the need of a personal encounter with the Lord Jesus Christ to know Him as Savior and Lord and then to have Him become the greatest reality in my life. He still is the greatest reality in my life.

At the age of 18, to learn that God had a plan for my

life, and that if I accepted His plan my life could count for all eternity was life-transforming. Ever since graduation from high school at 16 I was worried about all the graduates who would just waste their lives; I did not want to be one of them, but I didn't know how to make it any different until I heard that great pioneer, Dr. McQuilkin, explain that God had a plan for each life. And the plan included obedience to the command "go," to go until you were sure God was calling you to stay; and to pray every day to that end. I began to do it.

Then I heard another startling thing: Five hundred million had never once heard the name of Jesus. During that week I had already said, "Lord I want your plan" and "Lord I want to go if you will let me; show me where." And when I heard that five hundred million had never heard the name of Jesus, I said, "Lord, if it could please you, would you let me help some of those five hundred million hear the Word of God?"

So that was the way I began as a missionary—asking God, if it were His will that I might do that very thing. In the ordering of His steps, I got to Columbia Bible School and had the great privilege of studying under that pioneer, Dr. McQuilkin. What a heritage, nothing like it!

As a member of the Student Volunteer Movement, the first thing I had to do when I went there was to start giving testimonies in the various colleges in the area. I remember the first college I went to—Converse—for the socialites among the young women. There was a dress code and everyone came in evening dress to dinner. They all had a handkerchief hanging from their watch bracelets. I was from Philadelphia and so I went with a very marked Philadelphia reserve. I was taken aback as I walked down the steps to our first dinner gathering and heard those donned in their evening gowns calling out, "Hi daalin . . . , Hi shu-

gar . . . , Hi deaa . . . , Hi honey . . . . " And so I became
honey and deaa, shugar and daalin. And I'm so glad I did.
I'm a converted Southerner. The only thing I don't have is
an accent.

From Converse to the denominational colleges—like
Coker. And what a fence was up for anything like a Student Volunteer Movement group. But God gave openings
for such SVM ministry at the denominational colleges as
well as others.

Later I became a faculty member at Columbia and Dr.
McQuilkin's secretary (he hadn't had one before, so he
didn't know what he was getting into when he got someone who hadn't had any training!). As a faculty member, I
was able to do something on my heart—take students out
every weekend to a church or a college campus and let
them tell what they were learning of the Christian life
message and the call to missions. It was called student
deputations.

I know those from Columbia Bible College will never
forget those days of learning from Dr. McQuilkin who had
such vision, such gifts for teaching and communicating. He
would require us to answer the questions he gave us
every day saying "Be concrete, definite and specific. The
natural comes first, not the religious and pious answer." It
was hard to find the natural; you just wanted to be religious and pious! But oh how rewarding when you caught
the secret of seeing the Bible as a whole, that tremendous
progress of doctrine joining one book to the other with the
divinely inspired strain all through it. And what a joy to
have it opened up to you by a pioneer in communication,
who made the Bible come alive, which ended up in my taking a promise for every day from the Bible, and is a practice to this day. What a means of growth for the Christian.
How I miss it when I leave it out.

Student deputations was a way of students getting from Dr. McQuilkin what they gave out, a love for that which was nearest to the heart of the Lord Jesus—"those other sheep not of this fold" who have to be brought. And how we thank God that with the Student Volunteer Movement on the wane that the Student Foreign Missions Fellowship had its beginning with students. What a joy it was to work behind the scenes with Dr. McQuilkin on this vision.

The last great step came after 11 years of association with Dr. McQuilkin; there was always the cry from the Lord from the Keswick Conference, "Lord, if it please you, let me give to some group your Word, some of your Word in their language." After 11 years I knew more of what that meant. I had been out to Camp Wycliffe for about six weeks. It wasn't called Wycliffe Bible Translators then. It was the Pioneer Mission Agency meeting in Siloam Springs. I had just a small taste of it, but how wonderful it was. I thank God for those, including Dr. William Cameron Townsend, who started it all. And then in 1941 when the mission I joined applied for 99 passports during the second world war, mine was the only one granted—a serendipity for sure. Actually, it was something I had sought for. But then it was 77 days and nights on the ocean from New York to Massawa, Africa. Still another delay came when my partner Mary Beam was sent back to her own station at Doro, the first station in the tall grass jungle of the Sudan, a station Mary had helped to open.

Mary went back to Doro and I stayed in Massawa to help in the office. But I could trust the Lord for His perfect planning, because I had learned from Dr. McQuilkin that there are no parentheses in the life of a Christian.

Later I realized that part of the reason I had been kept there in Khartoum was that the Australian girl who had been assigned to be with me during the trip across had become so ill she had to be invalided home.

Just as the rainy season of six to eight months was beginning, with our nearest grocery store 500 miles away, the Mission was having a council meeting. Another serendipity was in store. The mission agreed it wouldn't be wise for me to live alone in that culture, even though another couple was there, who, by the way, also became ill and were invalided home. So they said, "We'll ask Mary Beam to come and stay with Betty for two years until we can get a replacement."

They never did get a replacement. Mary made a missionary out of me, and I thank God for that. And I'm thankful too for everyone who made up the Mary/Betty team: the churches, the prayer supporters and the Student Foreign Missions Fellowship at Columbia Bible College. They were all so much a part of us as we went out during the war. They all took part in helping us take over the stronghold that Satan had in Sudan, a stronghold he had possessed uncontested for so many centuries.

I just want to give you one picture of what it was like for us in Sudan. It was long after we had begun our work, when at the end of the dry season we saw some cars appear on the horizon. We didn't see many cars in our area because there were nothing but hand-cleared roads. These cars were full of four German psychologists from Heidelberg and all their gear. They said they were self-contained, and they came with sheaves of paper from the Sudan government. If you worked under the government there, you didn't do a thing without their permission.

We scrutinized their papers before welcoming the researchers, who were coming to do work among the Uduk tribe. They soon learned that Mary had built a little guest house they could occupy, and were glad to give up their gear and ability to be self-contained.

It wasn't even 10 days before they returned to us and said, "We can't get anywhere with these people. They just run from us. We don't know how you have any contact with them." They went on, "Could you give us at least two people to help us?"

We said, "We have only two who can speak any English. They are the only two we have had time to help with English." Mary and I were there because the government gave us permission to be there if we would teach boys to read and write in their own language. But then we got a burden for the little girls too and began a co-ed school, after two years of waiting upon the mission and the government for permission.

"We will be glad to give you these two," we said. "One is an Uduk by the name of Rasha. The other, Nyeru, is from a Berta tribe just six miles from the station." We explained that Rasha would not be able to communicate as well as Nyeru because he had not caught on to English as well. We also said he had a wife and twins. Rasha's twins had been born as a result of his prayer as a young Christian. He had asked God to give him twins to show his people that twins come from God and that they must not continue to bury them alive as they had been doing. That was all that we explained to them.

In less than a week, the German researchers were back. They said, "You've set us back in our research."

We answered, "We have? We're sorry. We're busy right now, but tonight we'll be glad to talk with you about it." And we went about our duties and routines and that night at about 10 o'clock we began dealing with the psychologists about their problem!

They began, "You told us that this man Rasha was a true Uduk, but he's not. We tested a group that are so many miles from the station and another group so many more miles from the station and in every one of them we have found a deep-seated fear that we have never found up to this time in our research. This man Rasha has not a trace of that fear, so he can't be a true Uduk!"

"Why is that?" we asked. "He can be a true Uduk, and we'll prove it to you."

"Now then, this man from the Berta tribe," the researchers went on. "We've found him to be a very unusual type of character." They said they had found something inside him like a violent anger boiling up that could explode at any moment. And the only reason it had never exploded was that Mary and I had used such wonderful "psychological" principles in dealing with Nyeru, who had once been a Muslim and was now a Christian.

So we began explaining night after night. Finally the researchers said, "Well, we must write a dissertation for publication on the effects of education in a primitive tribe. It is wonderful to think of what education can do."

As we thought about it, although we were not able to persuade the researchers with all of our claims of the resurrected Christ, we were thankful for how that resurrection power had changed our Uduks and our Bertas. Twenty-one Bertas and Chogos, two different tribes, had come to labor for us with their families. They lived among us, learned to read and write Uduk in our little school, were baptized by the church, and then went on to establish a small community. And just before we were asked to leave by the central government in 1964, the new converts said, "God is calling us to go back to our own country to establish a church by proclaiming what you have taught us." As a result two additional tribes were reached.

I want to mention just a few of the underlying constants in my look back at pioneer missionaries. As we tes-

If you don't go when God says go, you'll never have the inner vacuum satisfied."

tify on every campus and in every church we are privileged to go as area representatives of Africa Inland Mission, we are forced to face the reality that according to statistics millions are dying who are eternally separated from Christ. Now, it is God's command for all to go. And if you don't go when God says go, you'll never have the inner vacuum satisfied. We've had so many people come forward in meetings with tears streaming down their faces saying, "There was a time when I felt God saying to me, go. But I got married instead. I took a job instead and money got ahold of me." Oh, there are lots of excuses. The constant here is the power that exists for proclaiming the gospel—the power by which God raised the Lord Jesus Christ from the dead. And that is the very power we possess wherever we go as pioneers for Him—whether here or abroad.

Another constant is the message: Jesus as Savior and Christ as Lord. The goal is assured. "This gospel must first be preached," as constantly heard from Dr. McQuilkin, "and then shall the end come" (see Matt. 24:14).

A major in Bible, Dr. McQuilkin had a burden on his heart for the high school graduates who were going into secular colleges with unfed, dissatisfied hearts, who could easily be led astray from the truths so many of them grew up with in their homes. Dr. McQuilkin's answer was a major in Bible, a B.A. in biblical education. I was at Columbia Bible College during the years of getting that all arranged with the government. And then came graduate school. This was all part of the pioneering for the student missions movement.

Then there was the era of faith missions. The denominational missions had done a wonderful work in that area and continue to do so, but they tended to be located in the cities and along the coasts. The interiors needed to be reached. So more pioneering took place with Hudson Taylor and the China Inland Mission, the Sudan Interior Mission, African Inland Mission and others.

The Bible translation movement then proclaimed that each must hear the gospel in his own tongue. And how that concept went forward during that movement. Later Dr. Ralph Winter spearheaded the great movement known as the United States Center for World Missions.

I also remember the springing up of missionary conferences in various churches. Many of them started with the great World Congress in Detroit in 1941. That's when Mary Beam was asked to speak and invited me to come up to Detroit. A church at that World Congress for Missions accepted me for part of my support. As we look back, these conferences, emphasizing missions, giving missionary statistics, letting people get acquainted with missionaries all became a whole new movement. How we thank God for what He has done through the Urbana conventions.

Then, what about the burden for fellowship to get those committed ones to get to their missions destinations without being hindered. Isn't it sad that missionary giving hasn't caught on as it should? It sometimes takes a missionary two and a half years to get his support together. What a challenge to our churches! At Urbana '84, Dr. Eric Alexander called them the "napping churches."

The teaching and emphasis on missionary giving is so necessary if missions are to go forward. But there is also a new emphasis on the motivation for missions that has come during this period, the new teaching on the coming again of the Lord Jesus Christ, which I think had been neglected before this.

Looking forward I want to state a foregone conclusion:

It is still necessary to have pioneers for world missions. It's not all over! We need pioneers, even if they are serving in an advisory capacity.

What changes can we see ahead? Indigenous leadership, with the necessity of missionaries cooperating and praying for the leaders during this transition period, is one. We're learning from Greg Livingston and Frontiers Incorporated that traditional, as well as non-traditional missions, is important. Modern technology, radio and TV towers are sending out their messages in all directions and are covering much of the earth. But the hut in the isolated place with one or two working with a national to give each the Word of God in his own tongue is still an absolute necessity.

I want to close with a thought from Ezekiel 37. It's the picture of the valley of dry bones. The message came alive to me in our work in Kenya when we used the Billy Graham films in our itinerate ministry. We must have shown the film *His Land* 70 times.

How vividly the film portrayed those hard, white, brittle dry bones lying in the valley. And then through the Spirit of the Lord, the disjointed bones joined together, limb to limb. What did that picture show its viewer? The fulfillment of prophecy with the rebirth of the nation of Israel, which really came to pass in 1948.

I believe we can claim that promise for the 3 billion that have never heard the gospel. We are not meaning to insult those masses we love, but never having heard the good news, they are as lifeless as dry bones.

The power by which God raised the Lord Jesus Christ from the dead is yours and mine to enable us to pray for those pioneers still going out to share the gospel and give life to those dry bones. And they will live by the year 2,000!

5

My Excuses, God's Answers
by
Dan Harrison

I put my faith in Christ as a student at Bryan College in Dayton, Tennessee. I am deeply indebted to the Student Foreign Missions Fellowship there. Not only did I find new life in Christ, but I also found my wife, and together we felt God calling us to missions.

Actually some of my attitudes and motivation were changed only when I got involved in the SFMF activities. My eyes began to open. I saw a needy world out there, a world without hope, a world unreached. My eyes were opened because we had excellent missionary speakers and because we spent time in prayer. And throughout those experiences during two years at Bryan and later at Cornell, through InterVarsity, our life goals were modified. We worked through our excuses for not going into missions, and God provided our needs.

I can tell you it has been without regret that for 22 years my wife Shelby and I have served in missions for the cause of Christ. But that doesn't mean it hasn't been a struggle. In fact, we have had some pretty good excuses to stay at home.

Speaking of excuses, have you seen the Great Commission Exemption Form? It's humor with a point, a point that slips in between the fifth and sixth rib and stabs at the heart. (See next page.)

These types of excuses remind me of the farmer who went to his neighbor, who was also a farmer, and asked to borrow a rope. The reply came, "I can't lend you my rope. I'm using it to tie up my milk."

The farmer thought for a bit and then asked, "How do you tie milk with a rope?"

His neighbor replied, "When you don't want to do something, almost any excuse will do!"

How true. And isn't the same true for missions? When you don't want to do something, almost any excuse will do. Well, you've just read all the excuses, but none apply to you, right? Hopefully, some of the excuses and personal experiences I share will be of some help to you—an encouragement, a stimulus to think further, a challenge to action.

What About My Children?

Missiologists tell us that family and finances are the two most often heard excuses for not serving overseas. Our children's care and education are valid concerns. How will they be cared for? What about their education?

My own parents were missionaries—pioneer missionaries in Tibet. In those days Tibet was about as remote a place in the world as you could possibly be. At first, my mother taught my brother and sister. Then at ages nine and eleven they went to boarding school in central China. For that first year they had no contact with my parents. From there they went to another school in French Indochina, now Vietnam, with some missionary friends.

Travel back and forth from Tibet to Vietnam was next

Eternal Revenue Service
Great Commission Exemption Form
FORM NO. 0002

To be filled out by all who believe they qualify for exemption from Commandment Matt. 28:19 and Statute Acts 1:8:

_____

Your Name (Please type or print.)

_____

Present home address (number and street, apt. no. or rural route)

_____

City, town or post office, state and ZIP code

Check the appropriate box under which you claim exemption:

☐ 1. I am 100 percent disabled and unable to comply.

☐ 2. I have received nothing, therefore I can give nothing.

☐ 3. I don't like this Law—too much centralized power.

☐ 4. My neighbor doesn't comply.

☐ 5. I am applying for a 20-year deferment. I need time to think it over.

☐ 6. I recently completed a 20-year deferment and am applying for an extension.

☐ 7. My ship sails from Joppa at 5 tomorrow.

☐ 8. I have never gotten a personal call from the Boss telling me that this Law applies to me.

☐ 9. Since I did not qualify as a "child of God" under Eternal Revenue Form 0001 (and Law John 1:12), I am not under the jurisdiction of Commandment Matt. 28:19 and Statute Acts 1:8, and realize that I serve another master.

☐ 10. Other. Would you believe _____?

If you need more information about the Law of the Great Commission as stated in Commandment Matt. 28:19 and Statute Acts 1:8, please refer to subsidiary Statutes Mark 16:15; 2 Cor. 5:19; Rom. 1:1; Matt. 24:14; Mark 13:10; Luke 24:47; Acts 26:18; and Rev. 15:6. You will find all of these in the supreme government publication entitled "Bible," the handbook for all mankind.

Please complete and bring Form 0002 with you to your pre-heaven placement interview with the "Lord of Lords." He will then determine if you indeed qualified for exemption.

Please
Sign
Here   _____/_____
        Signature   Date[1]

We worked through our excuses for not going into missions, and God provided our needs."

to impossible. A letter took three months one way. So if Beth or Bruce wrote a letter to my parents, it was six months before the answer came back. Six months! So, naturally, if there was a problem, Beth and Bruce were not too keen to share it, because they didn't want to wait six months for an answer.

That was then, and simply doesn't apply today. Some children are separated from their missionary parents, but none need to be apart for any significant length of time. Better communication and faster travel have changed all that.

Some separation may be necessary, however. I know there are some popular Bible teachers today who claim that separation is simply not God's will. I would differ with that. I am convinced, based on personal experience and reading I have done, that the quality of the parent-child relationship on the field is fundamentally rooted in the quality time spent together, not necessarily the quantity of time.

The Scriptures are clear about the qualities we want to see in our children. Anyone who is in ministry should apply those criteria found in the book of Titus and elsewhere in God's Word to their own families. All of us want children who love the Lord. We want to see the principles of God's Word operating in our homes. That is our first line of witness, no matter where in the world we are located.

However, I believe it is going to be necessary for some of us to be separated from our children for some periods of time in order for the Great Commission to be completed. No, not the lengths of separation my brother and sister knew. I hope no one ever suffers that kind of separation again. But there will be times of separation, especially in some types of work and in some places in the world.

Kids often reflect their parents' attitudes. I have found

that missionary kids are very resilient. They respond well
to their experiences. One little girl said to me, "If Africans
are red and Americans are blue, I am green." But you
know, that gal felt good about being different. She is
stronger because she is different. And she was helped to
realize her advantages because she had had some extraordinary experiences. Her life had been enriched.

My daughter Paula graduated from Wheaton College
recently. She had a different set of values from growing up
in Papua New Guinea, where we served. She was able to
see the world through a different grid and understand life
in a way that many of her peers could not. What a privilege! She is now serving in China—teaching English, and
quietly witnessing to her faith.

What About Money?
Money is the second excuse so frequently heard. "Yes
Lord, I'll go, but I could never beg for money." Well, mission agencies don't want anyone begging for money. That
is simply not biblical. Matthew 10:10 says that the work-
man is worthy of his hire. That's true of people in any type
of ministry—from being a pastor, to being a campus
worker, or a missionary overseas.

I remember well when we finished up at Cornell University and went to the Summer Institute of Linguistics to
apply for service with Wycliffe. We got a letter from the
director in Papua, which asked us to come immediately.
We had six weeks to prepare. No one told us we couldn't
raise support in six weeks. We went to our pastor and he
called several of his seminary friends and told them about
us—commended us to them. He told them about what
God was calling us to do in Papua. Six weeks later we
were off to the field. We fully expected God to provide and
what do you know. He did! For 22 years now He has pro-

vided all of our needs, in every circumstance.

I remember in 1975 while we were on furlough in Southern California. We had come from the tropics, so I had no warm clothing. But I had a month's travel planned in the northeast part of the U.S. in the dead of winter. Shelby kept saying to me, "Dan, we've got to go buy you some warm clothes."

I said, "Yes, we must. What would you suggest we buy them with?"

She said, "Well, the Lord will provide."

I said, "Good!"

Now, I'd seen the Lord provide in some pretty unusual ways, so when she told me the Lord would provide, I listened to her. The day before I was to leave, she came to my office and said, "I think the Lord wants us to buy some clothes for you."

"How much did the Lord tell you to spend?"

"Oh, about a hundred dollars," she replied.

We didn't have that much to spend on clothes, I can assure you. But out we went and bought a nice looking gray woolen suit, a sport coat, a pair of trousers and two ties, all for a hundred dollars. The next day we received a letter from my nephew, who had no idea of our financial circumstances, except that he had heard God speaking to him. Enclosed was a check for $100 "for warm clothing."

We have family traditions in our home. And every New Year's Day we recount the record of God's faithfulness over the previous year. One time I said to the family, "Isn't it wonderful how the Lord has provided for us financially this last year?" Then I listed several specific ways in which He had done some unusual providing.

Holly, who was just six or seven at the time, said, "It's just as well for all the money we spent!" A marvelous response to the Lord's provision.

Ben is a 49-year-old Ph.D., whom we recently sent to China. Ben is a person who is used to teaching and receiving a paycheck for services rendered. I was talking to him about the Lord's provision for him. He said, "You know, I prayed and prayed about serving the Lord. I was willing to go, but not to beg for my support. I simply couldn't do that."

Then one day while Ben was preparing to go to China he was addressing envelopes to his friends into which he was going to insert a letter. As he did so he found himself thinking about that friend, praying for him, thanking God for the opportunity to be a partner with him.

He said, "All of a sudden the fear of the support-raising process just lifted and I realized the marvelous truth that is a partnership. Some send and some go. I am privileged to go and they are privileged to send. And they needed me just like I needed them.

"The Lord provided everything I needed financially. It was no problem. Now I am looking forward to sharing with my partners what God does through their prayers and money."

What a tremendous insight!

But there are all sorts of other excuses.

What About My Health?

And what about my family's health? How can I, as a responsible parent, take my kids into a country where there's a first-rate chance of getting a serious illness and where medicine is probably second-rate?

One Friday night in 1969, we had a party for teenage MKs. And unlike most other times, the kids didn't eat all the food we put out. They left some peanuts, which we forgot to pick up when we cleaned that night.

The next morning our 4-year-old daughter Paula began

eating peanuts. Then her little 19-month-old sister Melody came into the room. She began eating peanuts and then began to choke. We rushed her to the clinic. The doctor sent us to a hospital. But they couldn't help us and sent us to another hospital—60 miles away in our old WWII jeep. That trip took five hours.

At the hospital they pushed an adult bronchoscope down her windpipe, damaging her trachea. They ended up having to do a tracheotomy to restore her breathing. We went from there to the capital at Port Moresby.

Two weeks later the pediatrician said, "Mr. Harrison, I've run out of tricks. I don't know what to do for your child."

Every time they took out the tube, she couldn't breathe. Infection set in. We didn't know what to do next.

That day the Lord sent us a visiting doctor, a specialist in ear, nose and throat from the Mayo Clinic. He examined her and said, "That child is deathly ill. Get her to Australia as quickly as possible!"

We got on the next plane to Sydney. The doctor there tried everything. He too could do nothing. He told me, "Mr. Harrison, your daughter is gravely ill. We don't know how to solve the problem. She may be in intensive care for six to eight months."

Our hearts sank. I cried out, "Oh, God, God, what is going on?"

I'm going to leave the story here for a moment.

Two years later I was in Australia again. I met with Wycliffe representative, Ken Bradshaw. Ken welcomed me and said, "Have you ever been in Australia before?"

I responded that I had. "Oh, on holiday?" he inquired.

"No," I told him, "my 19-month-old daughter inhaled a peanut and we had to bring her here for care."

"Really. Was that about two years ago?" he asked.

I told him yes.

"Well, we prayed for you!"

I had to take hold of something to steady myself. I could hardly believe my ears. I had never met this man before and he was telling me that he and his family had prayed for my daughter.

I began to understand what must have happened, for in the middle of our conversation, we were interrupted by a telephone call for Ken from Melbourne. It was about a colleague, Carol Anderson, who had become ill. We stopped our meeting, of course, and prayed for Carol right then and there.

At the end of the meeting, Ken's wife Marilyn went to the phone. Underneath was a list of names and numbers as long as my arm. Marilyn called one after another and asked them to pray for Carol and her family. So, not only had the Bradshaws prayed for Melody two years ago, they had enlisted the prayers of many others.

Now back to the hospital. As you might guess, we were not at that hospital for six months. Ten days later we walked out with Melody. As we departed, the doctor asked, "It wouldn't do any good to tell you not to go back to Papua, would it?"

"No," I replied, "I'd probably listen, but I'd go back anyway."

He responded, "Well, I can't rightly tell you not to return."

We went back.

Melody took six months to fully recover. Today she is a beautiful 24-year-old woman. God completely healed her of the infection and looked after her needs.

Not only does God supply our needs, but He does it through a group of caring, loving, wonderful people—all over the world. They are God's family, the Body of Christ.

And, because of Him, they care about you and me.

God works in His own time. Our responsibility is obedience and faithfulness. Obedience to go and faithfulness in the task to which He calls. But there are plenty of excuses.

Why Not Stay Home?

There are plenty of needy people here too, so why do we need to go somewhere else?

Of course there are people in need here. But there are even more needy people in other parts of the world.

My parents went to China in 1921. After two years of language study they settled and ministered faithfully among the Tibetans, where I was eventually born.

My father was the only medical help available for perhaps a quarter of a million people. He set broken bones, sewed up cuts, pulled thousands of teeth and cured many venereal diseases.

My parents were energetic and highly motivated young people. Articulate and well-educated, before heading to the field they had offers of employment extraordinary for that day. But those opportunities were not the slightest bit attractive to them. They left home and family, and against the better judgment of some of their friends, they left the needs of the people of the United States for the greater needs of the unreached Tibetans.

Two years after they arrived in Hehtso, their first convert followed the Lord Jesus. The convert was a chieftain's son, an outstanding young leader by the name of Wande Ker. That young man's testimony radiated the love of Jesus Christ. My father and he would go out into the market; my father would preach and Wande Ker would give his testimony. People were moved.

But the Buddhists were concerned. And one of the

ways they showed their concern was by killing Wande Ker. His own neighbors killed him. Then dragged his body through the streets, as an illustration of what would happen to others if they followed these foreign ideas. It was a heartbreaking experience for my parents.

The mission suggested it might be best for them to move to another location. But because they were not instructed by God to move on, they didn't. It was grim going, but they hung in there. The fruit was slow in coming. In fact, after 25 years you could count the converts on one hand.

I remember sitting at my parents' table in Ithaca, New York, in the fall of 1961, while I was at Cornell. The mailman left an unusual letter, postmarked from India. It was from a Swedish missionary who had gone through a lot of trouble to locate Aka Sherup Jem Son, my father's Tibetan name.

As I recall, the letter started something like this: "Dear Mr. and Mrs. Harrison, We want you to know that all of your years of faithful service in Tibet has borne fruit."

The writer then went on to list by name a host of people from Amdo Province to whom my father and mother had ministered. They had become believers as refugees in India. God was faithful!

My parents prayed faithfully for China every day until they died. They lived with their bags packed, with the expectation that China would reopen to a witness for Christ.

Recently our daughter Paula came to us and asked, "May I take you to lunch? I'd like your advice on something."

We had no idea what she wanted to ask. We knew that she had a heart tender for God. We didn't know that she was going to ask for advice about going to China. I had been thinking about excuses, excuses that I have used and heard others use. And then God provided me with an opportunity to apply what I was going to say. At first I wasn't willing to give her advice. I was willing to tell her how I felt, but no advice!

"I'd love to see you home this year. You've been away four years. I'm looking forward to getting to know you as an adult."

Later we had lunch again. Paula said, "Mom and Dad, I feel called of God to go to China."

What could I say? Here was a prime opportunity for me to re-examine all my excuses on behalf of my daughter! Naturally I was concerned about her health. I was concerned about her finances. And I was concerned about her parents! I was able to re-examine those same excuses as they applied to my daughter going to China.

Somewhere in a remote corner of heaven, I can imagine my own parents peering through a window, watching their granddaughter Paula. And there is a smile on each of their faces—a knowing smile, pleased at her obedience, vision and faith.

Sure, we all have excuses. What are yours?

Note

1. Reprinted from *Pulpit Helps,* published by AMG International, Chattanooga, TN 37422. Used by permission.

6

The Levites: A Model for Missions Mobilization Today

by
David Bryant

We've all read in the newspapers about spies and counterspies who have been uncovered inside our own government. Some have been sentenced to three or four consecutive life terms in prison as a result.

I've had some exposure to what a secret agent is all about. Two years ago in the First Presbyterian Church in Winston-Salem, through no fault of my own and through a series of unusual circumstances, I found myself preaching to former President and Mrs. Gerald Ford. In the audience of 500-600 people, we had been told, were seven or eight secret service men.

In the earlier part of the service, I had fun sitting up on the platform trying to figure out who those secret agents were. But I never did. There's one simple reason for that. They look just like everybody else. They all wore suits and ties. I suppose if I had gotten up real close I may have noticed a bulge under the left shoulder, betraying a holster and gun. But from a distance, their silhouettes looked normal. They wore a friendly smile like everyone else that morning. Someone did tell me later, however, the best way to spot a secret agent: Everyone who is not a secret agent will be staring at the President; the agents will be watching the audience.

When I rose to speak that morning, I had a peculiar sensation, knowing that some out there looked just like everyone else, but embraced a whole different agenda in their hearts and minds, one that could lead to very aggressive action, if need be.

I get the same kind of feeling when I travel into churches and campus groups in this country and in other parts of the world today. I am more and more convinced that across the Body of Christ God is raising up what we might call "secret agents." They look just like everyone else. They're not any more spiritual, necessarily, than anyone else. In fact they may be struggling in certain areas and aware of those struggles in unique ways that almost drive them to be the agents they are. Yes, they look like all the other disciples sitting around them, but inside they're nurturing a whole other agenda.

One of the thrilling things for me over the last five years has been to articulate for these agents what this agenda is; what it means for God to place it on an individual's heart; what kind of identity they might assume accordingly; and how they move out with that identity and agenda for maximum impact on the global cause of Christ.

There is a biblical model for these secret agents—these quiet, unassuming, very routine mobilizers of God's people for their mission into the world. The term is *Levites*.

Levites and the Youth
One morning three weeks before Urbana '84, I was having my quiet time in Psalms.

The Lord says to my Lord, "Sit at my right hand until I make your enemies a footstool for your feet." The Lord will extend your mighty scepter from Zion; you will rule in the midst of your enemies. Your troops will be willing on your day of battle. Arrayed in holy majesty, from the womb of the dawn you will receive the dew of your youth. The Lord has sworn and will not change his mind: "You are a priest forever, in the order of Melchizedek" (Ps. 110:1-4, *NIV*).

The opening verse tells us the fundamental essence of world evangelization. Jesus has ascended, He is exalted on high, He is sitting at the right hand of the Father, He has been given all authority in heaven and in earth. And what is He doing there at the right hand this very hour? What He's been doing these past 2,000 years. He's transforming His enemies into His footstool. Or as Paul says in Romans 5:10: He's turning His enemies into friends. He's bringing them into such intimacy with Himself, that it is as if we are right at His very feet. And yet always aware that He is Lord, we are at His feet as a footstool.

Someday He's going to fulfill this to the uttermost in justice and glory, but right now He is doing it primarily by grace and redemption, through the gospel.

Then Psalm 110 goes on to say He extends His scepter in the midst of His enemies. I hear in that at least an echo of what today we call *church planting*. Whenever a congregation is raised up in the midst of a particular unreached people group, it is as if God unveils there in the midst of those who are His enemies a base of operations for His Kingdom. It's as if He sets up the throne of Jesus in the midst of a newly redeemed remnant of His people through whom Jesus can extend His reign in grace and redemption throughout that whole group of people.

These are all things God was showing me that morning in my quiet time. Psalm 110 says that when that vision is clearly understood—and it's a wonderful vision of hope— it will compel God's people to get with Him in battle. He doesn't want to be involved in this ruling and reigning by Himself; He wants us to be part of it with Him. As His troops, we become willing to join Him when we see what a glorious mission His day of battle is all about, and see that the victory is sure because it rests in Him.

He describes this army as being arrayed in holy majesty. How would you describe this army? First of all look at who they are following. How is He described as fighting the battle? He's fighting the battle first and foremost as a *man of prayer:* "after the order of Melchizedek." He's a king/priest. He has been permanently appointed to that position. For 2,000 years he has been ruling and reigning as a man of prayer. Therefore, I would assume that those who follow with Him into battle are themselves men and women of prayer, ready to fight the battle foremost as men and women of prayer.

The second clue is the phrase: "Arrayed in holy majesty," a phrase sometimes used to describe the vestments of the priests in the Temple—arrayed in holy vestments. The army is arrayed as Levites, as those who led the people into the holy of holies to seek the face of God. That's the kind of armor these troops are wearing.

As God brought this passage to me that morning in December, He seemed to say: "David, what I'm showing you in this passage is a drama that I'm going to reenact before you in a very significant fashion at Urbana '84." How so? Notice: The troops first mustered to follow this king/priest into the battle of prayer are the youth. You will first of all be accompanied by your youth, coming to you fresh and new like the dawn breaking over the horizon and like the freshness of dew on grass in the early morning. It will be the youth that will lead the way. Well, at Urbana '84, that audience was full of Levites. As you may know in previous Urbanas only a few thousand checked the box to become more significantly involved in daily prayer for world mission. But this time at Urbana '87 14,000 delegates checked this on the decision card. Furthermore, on the last day an ad hoc meeting was called at four o'clock in the afternoon to discuss prayer mobilization. Some of you who've been there remember what it's like after five days of Urbana intensity. To call for an additional meeting at four o'clock on the last afternoon to talk about mobilizing prayer on your campus—when there is packing to be done and friends to say good-bye to—would seem absurd. But almost a thousand students came to the meeting.

Afterward, we got in writing a thousand who signed up to express their desire to lead what we all call "support groups for missions" as a follow-up to Urbana. Really, they were nothing more or less than an effort to gather people to build their vision for the world, to spend extended times in prayer for that vision and then to hold one another accountable to be obedient to that vision. To do that, support groups were to meet at least three times in the spring for two and a half hours; the leaders would be required to lead them and then to send back reports to us about what God was doing as a result of each gathering. It was a fairly sizable commitment, but still a thousand students committed themselves in writing to give it a try. The Levites!

Yet as you read a book like *Campus Aflame* by J. Edwin Orr, which describes student revivals over the last 250 years and documents the impact that they have had on missions mobilizations, it becomes abundantly clear that the same common theme runs through those 250 years.[1] On the campuses, students have bound together as men and women of prayer, as Levites, if you will. And God has used them to mobilize His church-at-large with renewed vitality for world evangelization.

The Student Volunteer Movement was really a movement of Levites. Its major leader, John R. Mott, after returning from an extended tour in 1897, visiting SVM works in various countries of the world, concluded that the single greatest explanation for the vitality for the Student Volunteer Movement as he saw it in country after country was: "The concerts of prayer going on among students in each of these nations."

By the early 1900s there were over 47,000 students in this country alone involved in 3,000 mission study and prayer groups. Why? Because there were a few who were exercising the role of Levites, mobilizing many into active concerns as a kingdom of priests. Many of those 47,000 never made it overseas. Many of them were mobilized into the Laymen's Missionary Movement. But for all their impact, whether they went or whether they sent, world evangelization had its greatest expression in their life of prayer.

Dr. Wilbert Norton's recent book on Student Foreign Missions Fellowship called *To Stir the Church*,[2] clearly defines by its title what God's call to "student Levites" in all generations is about: It's to *stir* the people of God to seek Him, know Him, pursue His Kingdom, obey Him and be with His Son in missions in the midst of the nations.

I was in South Africa a couple of years ago for a consultation on frontier missions that brought together students from major denominations and racial groups, about 300 of us, to look at the theme of mobilizing prayer for a new mission thrust out of the church in South Africa. It was a bold vision for such a moment as this in the history of South Africa.

In the gathering was a young Indian South African from Durban named Thomas. At 18 years old, he had a God-given burden to see a revived church in South Africa sending missionaries around the world, especially from among his own people in the major urban center of Durban. God touched his heart very clearly about this role of a Levite, and he went back home to be one. He got together a group of people into a concert of prayer—that's what he called it. They began to pray for revival and world evangelization, until and shortly after Thomas was diagnosed with cancer. So the prayer group turned to pray for his healing as well. God did not see fit to heal Thomas; within a year Thomas was dead. But he left behind a tremendous legacy—a prayer movement still going, praying for a new kingdom thrust.

Shortly before he died, Thomas called his parents to his bed and instructed them that when his obituary appeared in the newspaper it was to tell his name and age, his address, his family members, and then to say only one other thing: that he was a part of the Durban Concert of Prayer. A Levite!

The Third Option
When we think about the unfinished task, we are full of such a mixture of feelings. Should I go? Should I send? Who am *I* in the midst of all of this activity? What am I to do next? For many years I answered these questions by describing all it means to be a world Christian, saying whether you go or whether you send you should first become a world Christian. I don't renege on any of that. But if I were to give you a more biblical term of what I've meant all these years by a "world Christian" I would use

Whatever other roles you assume, you can keep on being a Levite the rest of your life, and in so doing be assured God is using you strategically in the task of world evangelization."

the theme of the Levite. Instead of saying one either "goes" or "sends," I now like to say: The first choice you have is whether or not to become a Levite. Because whatever other roles you assume, you can keep on being a Levite the rest of your life, and in so doing be assured God is using you strategically in the task of world evangelization.

To be a Levite is to be a *fanatic*. Does that put you off a little bit? The last thing we think our campuses and churches need is another missions fanatic. When you study the Latin root of the word *fanatic* you'll find it comes from the Latin word *fanuum*, which means "temple." It refers to someone in the Latin culture so devoted to their particular deity that they lived in the temple practically all the time. Such people were eventually called fanatics— "temple dwellers." In that sense, the Levites were fanatics. Their whole focus was on the issues and the drama going on inside and around the Temple. They lived for what the Temple signaled about the purpose of God. So, they were fanatics.

I've come to the conclusion over the years that if we're going to see 3 billion people reached with the gospel, the Church has got to be flooded with fanatics, people who constantly dwell in the temple. We must have people who are given to seeking the face of God for themselves and for all the earth. They won't be more spiritual than anyone else, necessarily, though they may sense greater longing in their spirits. Willing to get out in front and set the pace in prayer, they will call to others, "Come, let us go together."

Some of our best friends are Levites! Moses, Aaron, Phineas, Zadok, Zephaniah, Jeremiah, John the Baptist, the apostle Matthew, the apostle Barnabas, Eli! Gordon MacDonald has shared about a man who "pulled switches" and "pushed buttons" to change his generation. That man—Eli—was a Levite! What's more, he was discipling a young man—Samuel—to become a Levite! Samuel's great ministry in the life of Israel, although he was a judge and a prophet, as many other Levites were, was as a Levite, who himself was discipled by an older Levite.

I was first introduced to the theme of Levites at Haystack '81, when IVCF commemorated the 175th anniversary of the Haystack Prayer Meeting. Some say that meeting spawned the Protestant missionary outreach from North America. One of the speakers for Haystack '81 was not able to make it, so at the last minute I was asked to give an address to conclude the whole conference as we gathered around the monument, which had been erected 50 years after the 1806 prayer meeting at Williams College in Williamstown, Massachusetts. We surrounded the monument—about 175 of us, many of whom were students on their way overseas to the mission field.

I had turned to the Lord earlier and asked: "What am I supposed to say?" Then one night before falling asleep, the words came: "What do these stones mean?" I had to rummage around in my Bible for awhile, but finally I came across Joshua 4. It was after the Israelites had crossed the Jordan. The river had been in flood tide, but now God had brought it in a reenactment of the crossing of the Red Sea. Afterward, God had 12 men of Israel bring up rocks out of the Jordan and pile them up, so that years later when their children asked them, "What mean these stones?" they could tell them about the day God opened the Jordan, brought them through and took them on into their mission for which He had called and redeemed them. That mission was to displace the enemies in the land and set up a base of operations for the Kingdom among the nations.

And I thought, *Yes, and that's what this monument is*

all about. What mean these stones? That's what this 175th anniversary is all about. Why were we commemorating a prayer meeting? So that the children of those who prayed might be reminded of what God did when he had six Levites meeting under a haystack. That's what those students were at Williams College: Levites. They had been mobilizing themselves and gathering others periodically for many months to seek God for revival on their campus, gradually expanding their agenda to include prayer for the world, particularly for Asia. God met them the August afternoon they prayed under the shelter of a haystack and out of that encounter came many prayer bands on other campuses in the ensuing four or five years, launching the modern Protestant missionary movement in North America.

I looked back to Joshua 3 and found that the reason Israel got through the Jordan River was because there was a band of servants called the Levites who lifted up the ark—the ark of the Lord of the whole earth—walked out in front of the people of God, and bravely marched right into the water. God told them not even to pause at the edge, but to go right on into the Jordan. That was quite an act of courage on the part of the people, but they went on and led Israel's mission.

First, the Levites held up the ark to remind everyone just whose mission it was. Then they marched into the Jordan, which had been their greatest barrier. As the waters parted, the Levites stood still in the middle of the river on dry ground. There they remained until the whole nation passed over. Finally Israel was released of its paralysis of fear in which it had lived for 40 years of wandering in the wilderness. Now the whole nation was mobilized to do what God had called them to originally do.

It was the Levites who broke the spell. After the

whole nation had crossed over, it was the Levites who came out last for the mobilizers were the last ones to head on into mission. But they had set the pace.

After Haystack '81 I began to dig into the Levitical theme even more. In fact when I was writing my second book, *With Concerts of Prayer,*[3] I did a word study on the phrase so often used to describe how the Levites stood *before the face of the Lord.* This phrase is used to describe the Levites in prayer, standing before the Lord on behalf and as a model for the whole nation. As I was completing my book, I suddenly stumbled onto Ezekiel 22:30, which reads: "I looked for a man . . . who would stand before me in the gap on behalf of the land . . . but I found none" *(NIV).* That had been the verse I had drawn from when I wrote the book *In the Gap:* "I looked for a man to stand in the gap."

This was God's great burden—how He was being perceived among the nations because Israel was desecrating His name among the nations. Not only was Israel spiritually and strategically vulnerable before their enemies, but they no longer had any credible witness to their enemies. So God says, "I'm looking for someone who will get into that breach and build it up. Someone who will restore the testimony. Someone who will again bring about what is needed in the spiritual life of God's people so they can be for me all that they need to be in the midst of my enemies, among the nations."

A world Christian, according to *In the Gap,* is a person who takes this call to heart, and literally orders his life day by day, whether he goes or sends, so that his whole approach to discipleship is ordered by a sense of being in that breach and doing everything to see it built up. But what I had not seen were the words *before me.* God is looking for someone, even if he doesn't come from the tribe of

Levi, who is willing to function like a Levite. He is looking for a Levite who will be a man or woman of prayer, who will stand before Him and build up that breach, not by physical stones, but by the "living stones" that Peter talks about in 1 Peter 2, which is a priesthood. And the best thing with which to build up the breach is people of prayer—a movement of prayer.

In many ways, such Levites are God's secret agents for advancing His worldwide purposes. Not because they are more spiritual, but because they are more focused on the heart of what God's mission for His people in the world is all about. They are *vanguards,* not for the purpose of revolution, but for mobilization. They are *pacesetters,* not by espionage, but by integrating the movement of prayer into the center of our lives together in the church. They are *catalysts,* not so much *for* the people as *before* the people. They are *models* of what the whole nation is to be, not as an elite core, but rather as an apostolic band. They are *way makers* blazing a trail into the presence of God and into the mission of God, breaking open the way so that others can come along with them.

Three words help define the role of the Levites as we see them in the Old Testament: disenfranchised, destined and devoted.

The Levites were the least likely people to mobilize God's nation into its mission in the world, because, in fact, the Levites had been totally *disenfranchised* over 10 generations earlier by Levi's own father Jacob. They were relieved of any inheritance in the land, because Levi, as father to the whole tribe of Levites, was a man of inexcusable fury and anger.

Later God converted their proneness to passion when the whole family of Levi became a people with fury and zeal for the glory of God. Of all the people you might have assumed God would lay His hands on within the life of His nation Israel, to let them be the pacesetters in a movement of prayer that would have international repercussions, the Levites were the least likely.

In any audience where I know there are secret agents, I assume in many cases they are the people who, if you were to take a poll in the congregation or in the campus fellowship, it will be assumed they will be the least likely to lead us in a movement of prayer. Often they aren't perceived as the "prayer warriors" of that group, though such consummate "pray-ers" are also desperately needed. But the Levites may have a role to play in terms of prayer *mobilization* that corresponds to their weakness. Their greatest strength in mobilization comes out of their weakness, their desperation, their sense of helplessness, their sense of need for the whole body to move with them into the work of prayer for spiritual awakening and Kingdom advancement among the nations.

Not only were the Levites disenfranchised, they were also *destined*—called by God. In Scripture we find an important principle demonstrated repeatedly: Faith is a gift of God; therefore prayer is a gift of God; and so praying people are a gift of God, and a movement of prayer is a gift of God. In this sense, the Levites were a gift of God. They came under God's specific mandate for them. If you study that mandate as expressed in Deuteronomy 33, you'll find that basically they were called to be "keepers of the covenant," the covenant made with Abraham, reaffirmed in the days of Moses, that God would bless His people and make them a blessing to the families of the earth. They were called to be the keepers of that covenant, to lead Israel in the fulfillment of *both* its dimensions. Deuteronomy 33 contains their "great commission," describing their destiny from the Lord.

Third the Levites were *devoted.* Their whole focus was to be on this process of mobilization. They were called a "wave offering." A wave offering was put before the Lord as a sign of thanksgiving and praise and in anticipation of the whole harvest up ahead. The Levites were devoted to the Lord in the same way. Their whole life was lived out to mobilize all God's people into a holy people, who by the very virtue of their life of seeking the Lord together would become His witnesses before all the nations. The Levites were a constant wave offering, a first fruits before the Lord of what God intended to make out of all Israel—a people who were also holy, devoted completely unto Him.

Furthermore, we read in Deuteronomy that the only inheritance the Levites had was the Lord Himself. Isn't that a wonderful thought? Now that's devotion! What kind of people will it take to really move the Church of Jesus Christ in the work of missions? We talk about sacrifice. We talk about forsaking all and following. In the end, what we need are people who in a fully positive way say, "My only inheritance is going to be you, Father. That's why I seek you and all that's on your heart. That's why I call others to seek you with me. Because you are all we have to make us the people you have called us to be and to fulfill the mission you have given us to fulfill. If we have this, it is enough!" In that theme there is hope for all of us whom God may be asking to perform a Levitical role, in principle, within our generation.

The ministry strategy God gave the Levites came in two phases: one was around the Temple, the other, among the nations.

Recently on the front page of the *Ashville Times* (July 2, 1986), there appeared a story about the oldest biblical inscription ever found in Jerusalem, recently uncovered and translated. The inscription is from Numbers 6:

This is the name that priests are to put upon my
people. "The Lord bless you and keep you. The
Lord cause His face to shine upon you and be gracious to you. The Lord lift up His countenance
upon you and give you peace." By this you priests
will put my name on the people and will bless
them. (see vv.23-27).

There it is, phase one of the ministry strategy of the
Levites as they ministered around the Tabernacle and the
Temple. What were they doing? Serving the seekers of
Israel. If seekers came up to worship, to seek forgiveness
and repentance, to offer first fruits of God's blessing, the
Levites were there to serve them and to take them
deeper with the God who reveals Himself to a seeking
people.

Furthermore, most of the Levites were scattered
throughout the nation. They didn't live in Jerusalem nor
around the Temple; they were scattered among the people
so they could constantly model what it means to live a life
that seeks the Lord. And they continued to put the name
of the Lord on their neighbors as their neighbors took the
model seriously and sought to integrate a seeking heart
into their own lives and occupations.

The Levites had a tremendous ministry: They were
leading the people to know the Lord as deeply as possible,
as deeply as the people themselves wanted to know Him.
Is there a need for people to fulfill that kind of role today?
Does it have implications for world evangelization?

In Madison, Wisconsin, we have a prayer movement
called Concerts of Prayer. We've been working at it for
almost six years now, and it has not been easy. But in
recent months God has done a new thing among us. Today

some 40 churches are represented by over 100 people gathered at any given monthly concert of prayer. We spend a whole evening praying for revival and world evangelization and in so doing we are putting God's name on our lives in a most dramatic fashion.

The key lies in the Levites in Madison. For about five years there was a little band of about 15 of us who pressed on in that role though it seemed no one else was ready to come along. But recently God has begun to call out leaders from the student world, from the missions world and pastors from churches. He's formed a leadership team of about 10 who are eager to say: "We are in desperate need to see God move in our churches and at our University in a new way, and we are willing to serve the Body of Christ in any way we're needed, as a leadership team for a prayer movement. As servants we want to help bring God's people together to seek the face of the Lord in this city that He might pour out His Spirit and do marvelous things that will not only reach our city, but reach out to the whole world in the end." Our band of Levites has multiplied itself into a whole host—over 100 from 45 churches and ministries who are out in front, setting the pace and leading the way, just like the biblical Levites.

Working "around the temple" had international repercussions! Phase one of their ministry was to the end (phase two) that God might be glorified throughout the whole earth through a people who had met Him, who knew Him, who lived daily in the fear of the Lord and in a constant desire to seek His glory, and who lived as a Levitical model before the watching nations.

Take, for example, Numbers 10. The Levites were given two trumpets to blow on two different occasions. One occasion was to assemble the Israelites into the Temple to worship the Lord or to seek council under His leadership. The second occasion was whenever the Israelites were to move on their journey into the land to carry out their Kingdom mission, or whenever they were to go into battle against their enemies. The same trumpets were used to move them in either direction, just as the same band of Levites were used to (1) keep worship and mission constantly before God's face and called all Israel to lay hold of God's victories in prayer, as (2) they did His work in the world.

Levites were a constant sign of Israel's redemption and calling to be a *kingdom* of priests. They also organized the nation for its initial mission. When they were moving through the wilderness (this is a beautiful picture of the Levite's ministry) it was only when the cloud or the fire rose at God's command, and the Levites rose up and folded camp in response to God's acting, that anyone else began to break camp and proceed forward. And when the whole nation was moving in its orderly form through the desert, the Levites, with the ark and sections of the Tabernacle, walked along, right in the center of the missionary procession.

Levites were setting the pace, leading the way, but they were doing so in the *middle* of the whole nation. What a testimony! The whole nation moving out is what the enemies of God saw marching under His faithful leadership to fulfill their mission. As the Levites acted as reconcilers, they modelled what it means to be ambassadors and peacemakers, even with those who sometimes are unclean or appear to be enemies.

Levites addressed the army before it went to battle, sounded the trumpets that headed the troops into battle, received the booty of war after battle as a worship gift to the Lord and in other ways linked up with Israel's kings in God's activities among the nations.

In a number of situations, they incorporated Gentiles into their ranks (you read about that in Joshua 9 for early on they were evangelizing Gentiles!). Furthermore, they identify with the "overlooked" (*hidden people* in today's missionary jargon), a number of times listed in the same classification as widows, poor, fatherless, lepers and foreigners. God was saying: "When you think of Levites, I want you to think of lepers, the unclean, the rejected, the disenfranchised, the foreigners. Let them be a constant reminder of where my heart rests and who I care about."

But overall you could say they preserved before an unbelieving world a credible and accessible witness to God's presence and holiness in the midst of Israel. And as a result, they opened the way for these truths to make a redemptive—evangelistic—impact in the midst of the nations.

The Levites were a continuous model of God's great commission for the whole nation to become a redemptive force of priests before all people. They fostered a worshipping community as the very base of operations for the advancement of God's kingdom throughout the earth. They provided a paradigm, or a picture, of how God would ultimately break through among the nations as He would build them into a temple of living stones, not situated on any given hill, but made up of all those, whatever people or tongue they might be, who seek God through Christ. They pointed toward the day when the whole universe would become God's temple so fully that a temple is needed no longer in that city. They were a paradigm of how God was going to bring about the climax of history.

Are such Levites needed today? Does world evangelization need people whose passion is for the Lord in a way that is a constant reminder of God's mission through His people among the nations? Do we need Levites to actually set the pace for that, to model it, to identify so much with it that when people are around them that's all they can think about as well? Do we need those who help the people of God where they need to be seeking the Lord for spiritual awakening and world evangelization so that the people of God can become everything that He wants them to be for His glory before the nations?

Look at them once more, and think of the Church today filled with such gifts from God. The Levites were forerunners, pacesetters, vanguards, catalysts, midwives, first fruits for the sake of the whole nation's calling as priests. Levites were not a super-spiritual elite, a diehard remnant, nor an ecclesiastical bureaucracy. They were raised up to be models for all believers, to emulate and duplicate in principle.

Truly they were the Old Testament's equivalent to apostles. They were the way makers who broke the ground for both the inward journey around the Temple and the outward journey among the nations. They fulfilled the commission in three ways. And these were the same three efforts we asked of the decision makers who joined the support groups for missions that formed across the country after Urbana '84: (1) by united prayer and praise for spiritual awakening and world evangelization, (2) by vision building both of the Lord and of His mission to the world, and then (3) by the accountability of obedience in a daily life-style. Those are the three key characteristics or tools that Levites have always had: their life-style, their life of intercession and the vision they keep giving to the people of God about whom all of us are and supposed to be.

Today, some of these modern-day Levites are going overseas. Others are going into sundry ministries in the Kingdom. But they're all committed, whether as goers or senders, to fulfill what I consider to be the most strategic role God could call forth as a gift to His Son, that is, to minister to the Church, wherever they are, as Levites. Because it's when the Levites are doing what God has called them to do that ministry enterprise will become what Christ has called it to be.

Notes

1. J. Edwin Orr, *Campus Aflame* (Ventura, CA: Regal, 1972)
2. H. Wilbert Norton, *To Stir the Church* (SFMF, 1986).
3. David Bryant, *With Concerts of Prayer* (Ventura, CA: Regal, 1984).
4. ———*In the Gap* (Ventura, CA: Regal, 1984).

7

Lay Mobilization for World Evangelism: Tentmaking
by
J. Christy Wilson, Jr.

Christian laity are God's secret weapon in the world. They represent His heavenly kingdom here on earth where Satan has tried to usurp the Lord's throne. And if the world is to be evangelized according to Christ's command, Christian laity as well as pastors and missionaries must be mobilized to complete the task.

More fully supported Christian workers are needed all around the world for they have been the means whereby God has planted churches and evangelized much of the globe. But over half of the people on earth today live in countries that do not allow fully supported missionaries. What are we to do about the people in these areas?

Mildred Cable, a wonderful woman of God who was with the China Inland Mission working in the Gobi desert, said, "No country is closed to God. If the front door is shut, try the back door." That is what *tentmaking* is: namely, lay Christians going into different nations with various professions, seeking to fulfill the Great Commission of our Lord Jesus Christ.

The one hundredth anniversary celebration of the Haystack Prayer Meeting was held in 1906 at Nashville, Tennessee at the Fifth Quadrennial Convention of the Student Volunteer Movement. A Christian layman who attended was so impressed with the way students were dedicating their lives to evangelize the world that he caught a vision of what laity could do. He started the Laymen's Missionary Movement in 1906, which spread like wildfire across this continent. In three years that movement established over 3,000 centers. They also pioneered prayer breakfasts for missions. In order to get whole congregations involved in missionary support, they started every-member canvasses in their churches. Thus they increased giving to missions by 400 percent in four years. Many churches still raise money through every-member canvasses, but have forgotten that the origin of this was for missions.

Numerous women's missionary societies were also established in churches. But today even though many of these continue, they have lost their original goal. According to Dr. Hendrik Kraemer, a great Dutch missionary to Indonesia, Christian laity are God's frozen assets. They need to be thawed out in order for the world to be evangelized.[1]

At the north pole there is a huge cap of ice on which the snow keeps building up. Scientists tell us that if that should ever melt, much of the world would be covered with water. In a spiritual sense, this is what will happen if Christian laity are melted with a passion for missions. In Habakkuk 2:14 we read, "The earth will be filled with the knowledge of the glory of the *Lord,* as the waters cover the sea" *(NASB)*. What is needed is to have dedicated lay people catch the vision and become effectively involved in worldwide evangelization.

The Scriptures teach the God-given principle of the priesthood of the believers. This truth was rediscovered at the time of the Reformation. And yet it usually has not been put into practice in Protestant or Catholic churches. This must be done before the evangelization of the world can be accomplished. First Peter 2:5 states, "You . . . are being built up . . . for a holy priesthood to offer up spiritual sacrifices acceptable to God through Jesus Christ" (NASB). Paul also states in Romans 12:1,2, "I beseech you . . . that ye present your bodies a living sacrifice . . . . And be not conformed to this world: but be ye transformed by the renewing of your mind, that ye may prove what is that good, and acceptable, and perfect, will of God" (KJV).

As believer priests we are to present our bodies as living sacrifices to God. The greatest thing we have to invest for eternity is our life. As the poem states, "One life to live, it will soon be past, only what's done for Christ will last."[2] The great missionary Robert Moffat said, "We have all eternity to celebrate our victories, but only one short hour before sunset in which to live them."[3]

What are you going to do with the life you are now living? Are you going to waste it for self? Or are you going to live it for the Lord, for eternity and for the evangelization of His world? When you get involved in worldwide evangelization, you find yourself in the current of God's power and blessing. Many Christians are playing in the eddies, alongside the river. But when you get involved in missions, the Holy Spirit sweeps you along with the wonderful tide of God's purpose and plan. Are you going to live just for this world, or are you going to live for the Lord Jesus? He gave His life for you, loves you and longs that you present yourself to Him as a living sacrifice to be a priest of God for eternity.

Tentmaking in Afghanistan

Even though at the time we did not realize it, our experience in Afghanistan proved to be a pilot project for Christian tentmaking.[4] In other words, just as the apostle Paul supported himself as a missionary by making tents, so we entered that country as teachers employed by the Afghan government. Fully supported missionaries were not allowed. But they wanted those who could help in the nation's educational system.

In 1951, I went to the Afghan embassy in Washington and was offered a contract to teach English in one of their schools. I told the ambassador that I had been ordained as a Christian minister; I didn't want them to think I had entered their country under false pretenses.

He said, "Since you have the teaching qualifications, we will be glad to accept you. Most of our teachers are Muslim priests. Therefore, it will be good to have a Christian priest teaching our young people." I signed the contract, and the Afghan embassy provided the money for my journey to Afghanistan. They also gave me a small salary while I was there. What a privilege it was to be paid to do the Lord's work while serving that nation in its education.

Over 70 Christians came into Afghanistan as tentmakers. Some were already there when we arrived. We had a marvelous fellowship. I was asked to be the pastor of the house church that was started there. As more and more came into Afghanistan and attended services, there was not adequate room in our home. There were no church buildings in the country since it was completely unevangelized.

In 1959 we heard that President Eisenhower was coming to Afghanistan on his Asian tour. Dr. Edward Elson had baptized the President after his election and before he was inaugurated. The President had come to Dr. Elson having known him as a chaplain in the army and said, "This job is too big for me without God's help. I have never been baptized. Will you baptize me?"

I wrote to Dr. Elson and mentioned that the mosque in Washington had just been built for the Muslim diplomats there. I requested him to speak to the President about asking the King of Afghanistan for permission to build a church on a reciprocal basis for the Christian diplomats and others in Afghanistan. President Eisenhower graciously agreed and asked King Zahir Shah about this when he was in Kabul. Permission was finally granted, and the new church was built and dedicated on May 17, 1970.

Now this was the time of the hippie movement. In one year, over 70,000 had come through Afghanistan, most of them American young people seeking for what they called "it." Through the help of Youth with a Mission, we were able to start a ministry among them called Dilaram, which means "people of heart." Many of these hippies came to Christ. We would have 40 to 60 of these world travelers in each of our services in the new church. But because some Afghans also attended the services and were converted, the Muslim government expelled some of us and destroyed the church building during the summer of 1973.

Twelve Types of Tentmakers

It was while we were in Afghanistan that I realized we were self-supporting missionaries the way the apostle Paul was, and the idea of tentmaking took formation. But then I also came to see that there are approximately 12 different types of tentmakers.

One. The first kind includes every Christian, just as in one sense every believer is a missionary. Some hold that only those who are cross-cultural witnesses are missionaries. Webster's Dictionary lists 63 different meanings for the word *of*. Therefore it is easy to have at least two different meanings for the word *missionary*. It depends upon whether you are speaking of every Christian as a witness or are referring only to those who are cross-cultural communicators.

Jim Elliot, who was killed by the Auca Indians, wrote, "We don't need a special call to be a missionary, we need a kick in the pants."[5] He held that every Christian could be a missionary. On the other hand, Peter Wagner, in his book *On the Crest of the Wave* states, "Not every Christian is a missionary." He adds that only a low percentage of believers have the missionary gift.[6] Who is right?

In a real sense everyone who is a born-again Christian is a witness for Jesus, whether at home or abroad. But on the other hand, there are certain ones who have a real missionary gift to motivate and facilitate others. Paul says in Ephesians 4:11,12 that when Christ ascended to heaven, He gave the Church gifts of five kinds of leaders. The first are called apostles. These can refer to missionaries because the Greek word *apostello* means "to send," and the Latin word *mitto* also means "to send." It is from the word mitto that we get missionary. In Acts 14:14 we read of the apostles Barnabas and Paul where this title is used for them as missionaries. There are also the 12 apostles who were especially chosen and "sent out" by our Lord. But besides these, there were the missionary apostles who were a gift to the Church. This did not mean that they were the only ones who were to evangelize or to plant churches. Paul and Barnabas were initiators and facilitators who, when they had led people to Christ, got them to evangelize others and plant new churches. Thus certain ones have the gift of being motivators in missions.

But in a real sense, all Christians should be missionaries. William Carey brings this out in his book *An Enquiry*

The Great Commission applies to every Christian. This is also true of all believers regarding tentmaking, since they should be witnesses for Christ whatever their jobs may be."

into the Obligations of Christians to Use Means for the Conversion of the Heathens.[7] There he demonstrates biblically that the Great Commission applies to every Christian.

In the Reformation it was generally thought that Christ's command applied only to the 12 apostles. But Carey argues that if that were the case, the Church of his day did not have the right to baptize, because in Matthew 28:18-20 the command to baptize is right along with the command to evangelize. He also brings out that Christ said, "And, lo, I am with you alway, *even* unto the end of the world" *(KJV)*. Carey pointed out that the apostles did not live to the end of the world. Therefore he concludes that the Great Commission applies to every Christian. This is also true of all believers regarding tentmaking since they should be witnesses for Christ whatever their jobs may be.

Two. Christians at home can be cross-cultural witnesses as they minister to internationals who have come to where they are. For example, the church that we attend sponsored an international student conference. We were assigned a Muslim from Mecca who was studying engineering at Harvard. One day at four in the morning, he knocked on our bedroom door. He said, "Excuse me for bothering you. But it is time for me to pray, and I don't know where to face toward Mecca. Will you please show me the right direction." I had to do some quick thinking to point eastwardly. What an opportunity we had right in our own home to witness for Christ to one who had come from the strictly closed religious center of Saudi Arabia.

Three. There are tentmakers with various mission agencies who get positions in universities or other institutions and receive a salary. They are regular members of mission boards. But they get jobs and usually return what they earn to their agencies.

Four. There are those who purposely prepare to be tentmakers and go to closed or restricted areas like mainland China. These often are recruited and orientated by Christian agencies.

Five. There is a great opportunity for Christians to go abroad to study, even to get doctor's degrees, and to be witnesses for the Lord Jesus Christ. So there are student tentmakers. So far very few evangelicals have taken advantage of this form of witness by enrolling and studying abroad.

Six. There are openings for tentmaking teachers around the world. When my wife and I were in mainland China, we met an English teacher who had been invited to give a series of lectures on Western culture. At Easter, she spoke about the meaning of that celebration. She told how many Westerners believed God had become a man in Jesus Christ, had lived a perfect life, had been killed as a sacrifice for the sins of the world and had risen from the dead on the third day. Not only was the whole university out to hear this lecture, there were faculty members sitting in the front rows. Her presentation was taped and broadcast over radio Shanghai so more people could learn about the meaning of Easter in Western culture and also get practice in English.

Seven. There is a great opportunity for tentmakers as Christian business people. (That is what Paul was.) By having believers working with multinational corporations, unfair practices that oppress poor people can be restrained.

Eight. Christian tentmakers can also serve around the world as government officials or as workers in secular agencies. Our daughter and her husband are in Port Moresby, Papua, New Guinea. He has his Ph.D. in public health and is working with the World Health Organization of the United Nations assisting that country medically. But their main purpose is to be there as self-supporting missionaries for the Lord Jesus.

Nine. There are also tentmakers who go abroad as short-termers. Tens of thousands of Christian students go abroad every summer to assist missionaries in their fields of service. This is a new development as travel used to take months to get to different countries and it was not possible to make a round trip in a short time the way it is today.

Ten. Christian retirees can also serve as tentmakers. One couple who had retired from General Electric came to Afghanistan. They spent 10 years there serving the Lord. The Social Security Administration would not believe that anyone would retire and go to a place like that without getting a huge salary. Therefore, they refused to give them their allowance, until a Christian lawyer convinced them that they really were retired there.

Eleven. Christian pastors have an opportunity to be tentmakers as well. At one Urbana Student Missionary Convention, a minister stopped me in the assembly hall. He said, "I brought young people from my church so they would get a missionary vision. But I have been bitten by the bug myself. Is there anything a pastor can do on the mission field?" I told him about the hundreds of English-speaking churches all over the world. He asked me for the address where he could write to find out more about this. Later I received a letter from him in Panama where he is serving an English-speaking congregation. His church there has also experienced a spiritual revival. He and his wife live right on the Panama Canal and distribute the Scriptures in various languages to sailors from all around the world. He is not funded by people at home, but is supported by the congregation in Panama, made up of different tentmakers who are serving the Lord there.

Twelve. Finally, there are the international visitors. As they are led to Christ, they return to their countries as tentmakers. A Muslim dentist who studied in the United States came to the Lord and since returning to his country has led over 40 Muslims to Christ.

Tentmakers Need Training and Backing

There are tremendous opportunities for lay people to be involved in world evangelization, but they need training. Mission agencies usually require candidates to have at least one year of Bible. Tentmakers also need training in the Scriptures. No matter what their profession, their real vocation will be to share Christ as revealed in God's Word. William Carey said that he fixed shoes for a living, but his real profession was that of being an ambassador of Jesus Christ.

Furthermore, it is essential for a tentmaker to be associated with a mission agency if his or her ministry is to be successful. More and more boards are establishing branches for tentmakers. For example, self-supporting witnesses going to China can be greatly assisted through their being associated with a mission agency. It can help them with their orientation, language learning and fellowship on the field. When my wife and I went to mainland China, our tour group had a Christian couple who were in charge of personnel for their mission agency. They had different ones working in China, and so they visited them, talked with them, encouraged them and advised them. A mission board can also assist tentmakers with their "re-entry shock" to their own country and help them secure another position.

At the Lausanne Congress in 1974, when an opportunity was given to make suggestions, a Christian businessman by the name of Ford Madison stood up. He said, "What can we Christian laity do for worldwide evangelization? Most of our pastors want us to come to services regularly, to give our tithes and offering faithfully and to be involved with the program of the local church. But we want to do more. We want to be taught how to lead people to Christ, how to live the victorious Christian life, how to disciple others. We want to be involved in the strategy for world evangelization."

Thus, at Lausanne II, in 1988 the place of laity in completing Christ's commission is to be a central focus. Ford Madison, who himself was a tentmaker in Central America, has been asked to head up the planning for this segment. He has secured a Christian researcher who has located 128 evangelical lay organizations, or affinity groups, such as Gideons International, the Christian Businessmen's Committee, Women's Aglow, the Full Gospel Businessmen's Fellowship International and others.

Lay mobilization for world evangelization can be the wave of the future. How are you going to take part in this great move to complete Christ's commission?

Notes

1. Hendrik Kraemer, *A Theology of the Laity* (Philadelphia: Westminster Press, 1958) pp. 9,10.
2. Taken from a Christian plaque.
3. Taken from *Living Quotations for Christians*, edited by Sherwood Wirt and Kirsten Beckstrom (New York: Harper and Row, 1974).
4. This is described more fully in the two books by J. Christy Wilson, Jr., *Afghanistan—the Forbidden Harvest* (Elgin, IL: David C. Cook, 1980) and *Today's Tentmakers* (Wheaton, IL: Tyndale Press, 1985).
5. From a lecture given by Jim Elliot at Gordon-Conwell Theological Seminary on January 22, 1986.
6. Peter C. Wagner, *On the Crest of the Wave* (Ventura, CA: Regal, 1983).
7. William Carey, *An Enquiry into the Obligations of Christians to Use Means for the Conversion of the Heathens* (Leicester, England: Ann Ireland, 1972).

8

A Personal History of the Early Years of the Student Foreign Missions Fellowship

by
H. Wilbert Norton, Sr.

Nearly 50 years ago I used to sit over here on the right side of this very auditorium; it was during summer school in 1937. Dr. H. Framer Smith was our professor. He taught Romans at evening sessions. Every evening just as the sun was dipping below the farthest mountain range, he would pause for two or three minutes as the class furtively peeked at the sunset instead of paying attention to him. He was one of those "old school" professors who expected his students to look at him as he enunciated and outlined each lesson specifically, so he would pause and give us time to look at the sunset! Similarly, I want to give you just a little bit of time to see what God has created in the Student Foreign Missions Fellowship. It's beautiful! His creation—in this place, Ben Lippen, 50 years ago.

Early in the history of Ben Lippen only the iron structure was here. When we students returned the next year we found all of this beautiful stonework. We returned again and found that the sawdust underfoot was gone and a permanent floor was installed—gradual improvements.

These are Ben Lippen memories of half a century at the founding conference of the Student Foreign Missions Fellowship.

The steel structure of this building originally came from the old post office in Asheville, which was hauled in during the Depression. This information provides the frame of reference for the early development of the SFMF for World War II missionary living—how to use "leftovers," or using what is available.

The Ben Lippen Conference Inn, in a sense, is a model for missionary living, prior to its destruction by fire some years ago. During the 1936 conference session, there was neither enough money nor time to finish the walls between the rooms. Consequently heavy construction paper, the kind builders use on the floors of new buildings, was used for the walls. The walls of the Inn were actually constructed of paper!

Take a moment to listen to the birds as they sing their evening song! Every once in a while I like to pause for "sound identification." The same Creator of the Smokey Mountain sunsets and the beautiful even' songs of the birds is Jesus Christ, "The same yesterday, today, and forever" (Heb. 13:8, *NEB*). He is the reason we are here for Celebration '86.

History is a dilemma, if not a disaster, for most students and most students' parents and their pastors. We seldom take time to observe what God our heavenly Father has been doing in history to encourage us in our present-tense living, as we seek to exegete the Scriptures and encourage Christians to grow in grace and knowledge of the Lord Jesus Christ.

We observe the grace of God in the past and how He's worked to bring us to the present. We are filled with expectation of what He will be doing in and through us in

We observe the grace of God in the past and how He's worked to bring us to the present. We are filled with expectation of what He will be doing in and through us in the future."

the future. The Lord Jesus taught us to pray, "Your kingdom come, your will be done on earth as it is in heaven" (Matt. 6:10, *NIV*). This is our goal, our purpose. This is what the Student Foreign Missions Fellowship has been all about. The events of the past must be compressed, difficult though it may be.

The personalities participating in our Celebration '86 have sought diligently to relate to us the history of God's working in the past. We follow Gordon MacDonald's model when we refer to the beloved Cambridge University saint, Simeon, and his influence over those decades in the eighteenth century at Trinity College, the beginnings of the InterVarsity Movement.

Christy Wilson, Jr., in his humble view of himself has from time to time attributed to me some of the success of Toronto in 1946. But it was he who supervised the total activity. I respected him, fulfilled his commands, doing what he ordered. Thank God, I was obedient!

Dave Bryant already in this Celebration has been seeking to make Levites out of all of us, relating the committed priesthood of the Old Testament.

A very significant part in the SFMF was played by Elizabeth Cridland. At this celebration we stood before the television camera singing, "How Great Thou Art," with the choir behind us. In the spring of 1937, as she directed a team of students engaged in a weekend of meetings, we also sang together in a church in Wilmington, North Carolina. In my nervousness, all of a sudden I slipped into something that approximated the tenor part while she was beautifully singing the alto. Since then we have not sung together until this evening. Historically all this ties in with my first visit to Ben Lippen in 1936 and the founding conference of the Student Foreign Missions Fellowship.

Just outside Huston Hall a college student introduced

himself as Anderson. I looked at him. Anderson? I had what my Lingala friends in Zaire call *Intembe* (doubt) in my heart. I looked at him again. He was a Southern Anderson. I soon discovered that the Johnsons and Andersons in the South are Scots. I was beginning to break out of my very provincial, ethnic Swedish background.

Church and mission historians generally do not tell us about the great nineteenth century missionary thrust that came out of Scandinavia. At the end of the eighteenth century and the beginning of the nineteenth century, spiritual revivals brought also a revival in hymnody, producing such hymns as "How Great Thou Art," replacing the traditional intoning of the Psalms at the Sunday services.

The nineteenth century Scandinavian revival movement provided the background for my forebears who emigrated to this country and brought the gospel with them to the Swedish, Norwegian and Danish communities in the United States.

In this cross-cultural experience at Ben Lippen I found Jesus Christ to be the same changeless One as I began to adjust to the many new Southern cultural niceties. A little fellow was next to me in the dining room of the Inn one day. I introduced myself as Wil Norton. He said his name was "Omah Bane."

I said, "Nice to meet you." I saw him again at noon and asked, *"What* is your name?"

He said, "Omah Bane."

I asked him, "Where are you from?"

"Charleston."

I don't know how many times I saw him during the week and each time I asked, "What is your name?" Finally he spelled it out, H-o-m-e-r P-a-y-n-e.

This was the beginning of my cross-cultural experience, topped with turnip greens, hog jowl and all the finer things of Southern living. The newspaper headlines in Columbia, South Carolina announced to the world the answer to the reporter's question asked of the governor, "What is your favorite food on New Year's Day?" The governor answered, "Hog jowl and black-eyed peas!"

The impact of this new life-style was awesome, coming as I did from a very restricted Swedish background. I might just as well have come from the Ngbakas of the northwestern corner of the Ubangi district of the then Belgian Congo. It was all so shockingly new to me.

One of the purposes of the conference at Ben Lippen was to consider the advisability of establishing a new student missionary organization.

Dr. Robert C. McQuilkin had spoken on two occasions while I was a student at Wheaton College. The second time was during my senior year in February, 1936. He had a unique message and presentation. Shortly after the series of services began, however, Dr. McQuilkin became ill.

The weather was bitterly cold. As I recall, he needed a heavier overcoat. Someone helped him into a downtown Chicago department store to purchase a new coat, but it was undoubtedly too little, too late. He was confined to bed with a bronchial infection that lasted for a couple of days.

During his absence, a substitute preacher assisted in the service, Dr. Walter Wilson, the founding president of Kansas City Bible Institute. Dr. Wilson was a prodigious evangelist who had published a number of books recounting his personal experiences. He led many people to personal faith in Christ.

Suddenly one of the senior men in the front of the chapel, Don Hillis, the pastor of the Tabernacle Church in Wheaton and a graduate of Biola, asked the question, "Dr.

Wilson, what does a Wheaton student have to do to be filled with the Spirit?"

Don said that Wheaton students were very conservative and were apprehensive about being filled with the Holy Ghost. Then it happened. Another student stood up. It was as though a dam had broken and the water was rushing through the break. Other students stood and asked God's forgiveness. They tearfully asked the faculty and their peers for forgiveness for things said, for acts committed and attitudes they knew were wrong. The campus was stunned.

Initially President J. Oliver Buswell was unsure of how to handle the situation. Then a young college president who became one of the great reformed theologians of our era, Buswell led us into a new appreciation of the reality of God's sovereignty. God was indeed sovereign throughout the entire day. The dean of men, who was also professor of geology, testified, "I have prayed for this for 20 years." Revival had come to Wheaton College! The Holy Spirit was ministering to students and faculty alike.

Dr. McQuilkin recovered sufficiently to conclude the week of meetings. His series of messages generally followed after the Keswick emphasis beginning with teaching on the doctrine of sin, continuing on salvation and how to live the Christian life, concluding with Christian service. The last day was devoted to emphasis on missions.

Dr. McQuilkin was a student of human nature. He knew how to communicate. At the close of the service he would ask those who had already volunteered for overseas service as missionaries to stand up. Then he would say, "Perhaps you have never thought of being a missionary and you do not yet feel that God has called you, but you are willing to pray about it until you know; will you join those who are standing signifying that you will pray for

God's guidance in regard to missionary service?"

As a 15-year-old high school student, six years before, I knelt alongside my bed one night, the battle raging in my teenage heart, Should I be a lawyer or should I be a preacher? Finally I said, "OK, Lord, if you want me to be a preacher, I'll be a preacher." But I had never considered the missionary option. A high school friend of mine, I thought, would make an ideal missionary, but I had never seen myself in that role. However, that night at the conference I reasoned, "Well, that's the least I can do." So I stood up, committing myself to pray until I knew God's will. That was the beginning.

God will guide us when we ask Him. When we covenant with Him publicly the consequences are serious.

As Dr. McQuilkin concluded, he informed us that a graduate school of Bible and Missions would open in September 1936 at Columbia Bible College.

I had been considering various seminaries—on the East Coast, just over the border in the South, and still another in Texas. I was deeply impressed by the Christlikeness observed in Dr. McQuilkin, a man who knows Jesus. He knows how to talk about Jesus. He knows how to share Him. He knows how to lead people on to understand Him.

Other seminaries have their libraries, they have facilities and faculties. But this man has something unique in his knowledge and presentation of Christ. I wanted to get as close to him as possible. So I enrolled in the first class of the graduate school of Columbia Bible College.

The Student Conference at Ben Lippen was actually my introduction to my seminary experience. Some of the students at Wheaton, after the revival, had begun talking about missions. The Student Volunteer Movement had existed on the Wheaton Campus since the visit of Samuel

Zwemer in 1887. The SVM at Wheaton, however, was lacking in dynamism in the early 1930s. Not very many came to their prayer meetings. Nor was there very much in-depth understanding about the SVM.

Jimmy Belote, a graduate of Columbia Bible College, transferred as a senior to Wheaton for his B.A. degree and was a leader for some of the discussions on missions. He said, "We need to call all the missionary students together and do something." The result was a delegation going from Wheaton to Ben Lippen for the 1936 Student Conference.

Meanwhile at Columbia Bible College a strong student missionary movement already was active on campus with Joe McCullough as the chairman. When we met at the 1936 Conference to discuss these matters, Joe McCullough was elected acting chairman. He was then elected to represent the Ben Lippen students at the Keswick, New Jersey conference there the following week. The two student groups determined that a new biblical evangelical student missionary movement was needed. Reports of activities of the Student Volunteer Movement were seriously reviewed, evaluated and the decision was reached for forming the Student Foreign Missions Fellowship.

These were the years of grievous financial and economic depression. There was no money available to sponsor a new student missionary movement. But that did not deter us. We knew we could pray—and pray we did! As we deliberated about the future of the Student Foreign Missions Fellowship, we prayed about our needs specifically, and God provided.

Ken Hood, also Wheaton '36, and I enrolled in the Graduate School of Columbia Bible College, bringing with us the student missionary experiences of the spring semester at Wheaton. He and I were roommates at

Columbia. As we discussed the student missionary developments, several of us felt we ought to visit other colleges to share the facts with their students and faculties. This was not an effort to imitate the early Student Volunteer Movement. Actually we were unaware of the early history of the SVM. We were responding instead to what we understood as God's leading.

How did the Columbia Bible College administration react to such a suggested trip? They loaned us a car, without any mileage charges. The students, faculty and staff prayed and took up an offering, giving an opportunity for everyone on campus to share in the effort. We visited Bob Jones College, Moody Bible Institute, Wheaton College, and Mary Baldwin College in Staunton, Virginia, where a Virginia State Student Volunteer Movement was meeting that weekend. The strong emphasis of the SFMF in its beginnings was "to stir the church to the pressing obligation to make Jesus Christ known."

There was also a very strong emphasis on the Church to help the Christians respond to their mandate to evangelize the world. We were unaware of the impact of the Haystack Prayer Meeting and the founding of the American Board of Commissioners for Foreign Missions, the first North American missionary agency. It was the early nineteenth century student missionary volunteers who stirred the churches. That is all we were seeking to do in the midst of the impossibilities created by the Great Depression of the 1930s. We had no role models to follow other than Hudson Taylor, "Praying" Hyde, George Müeller and others like them.

Subsequently a second student missionary trip was made in the summer of 1938. Meanwhile Joe McCullough had gone to Bolivia. He was acting secretary of the Student Foreign Missions Fellowship until he graduated. He served for one year before he left for Latin America. His mantle then fell on me and I became the acting secretary. We had no budget, but we knew we had the Lord, so we made our student missionary trips as the Lord provided. Our burden was "to stir the Church." So we pooled our personal resources and prayed. God provided us with enough money for Ken Hood to "go up North," after our final exams, where he bought a Model-A Ford with four doors and four wheels on it. The team met him right here in Ben Lippen after he made his used car purchase. The price of our car—$125!

On the night of our departure we met with Dr. McQuilkin in his summer cottage. He prayed for us and with us. At 2:00 A.M. our team of five took our places in the old Model-A, the running board loaded with suitcases covered against the elements with oilcloth. Our team included Ken Hood, Lewis Bates, Davison (Dixie) Philips, William Barnett and myself.

We had only six meetings confirmed over the six weeks—a very dangerous undertaking. God had given us our first meeting in Washington, D.C. Our reasoning: If we have the first meeting there, we'll go on to the next one, wherever it is. We were literally, "trusting the Lord." Out of six weeks of travel we had only one night without a meeting. And we were grateful to have one night free out of six weeks! The Lord indeed supplied every need.

When the tour concluded, every team member received enough money in Chicago to pay for his return home. That is the basic story of the faithfulness of God in the early years of the SFMF. It underscored the reality that Jesus Christ is, indeed, the same yesterday, today and forever.

Of the first executive secretaries, Joe McCullough was from Columbia Bible College, along with myself, Ken

Hood and Neil Hawkins. Pete Stam was an alumnus of Faith Theological Seminary and Herb Anderson studied at Princeton. And all but Joe were alumni of Wheaton. Columbia and Wheaton made a significant contribution to the early beginnings of the Student Foreign Missions Fellowship.

The first five of these executive secretaries all departed for their respective mission fields creating a breakdown in leadership continuity. Consequently a new strategy was needed.

In the meantime, the InterVarsity Christian Fellowship had labored in the U.S. from its base in Toronto. An Australian by the name of Stacey Woods, a graduate of Wheaton, had studied at Dallas Theological Seminary before coming to Wheaton, receiving his baccalaureate degree in 1934. We were on campus together. Stacey had been called to Canada to become general director of Inter-Varsity there. A classmate of Ken Hood and myself, Charles Troutman, had been interested in student work and joined Stacey in Canada. Stacey had begun to express his concern that the Canadian InterVarsity did not have a concerted missionary outreach. A letter was sent to Neil Hawkins of the SFMF in 1941 suggesting the possibility of discussing this need. In the meantime InterVarsity was begun in the U.S. under the leadership of Stacey Woods.

Finally in 1945 a joint committee had implemented the merger of these two organizations. Among those on the SFMF joint committee were Dr. Paul Culley, dean of men at Wheaton College and later professor of missions at Columbia Bible College, Don Hoke, assistant to the president at Columbia Bible College, Peter Stam, then a missionary candidate with the Africa Inland Mission, now its U.S. director. Don Hoke went to Japan with his wife Martha as missionaries with the Evangelical Alliance Mission to found the Tokyo Christian College. They were all on the move with the gospel to the ends of the earth. Herbert Taylor, president of Club Aluminum, a manufacturing company of kitchen cookware in Chicago, was chairman of the Board for InterVarsity. He and Stacey Woods represented InterVarsity on the merger committee. This merger was effected in the summer of 1945.

Who now would provide the student missionary leadership? For five years, during that whole World War II period, my family and I were in Africa. We had returned exhausted to the U.S. in July 1945. By then my weight loss had reduced me to 127 pounds of weary missionary flesh.

Shortly after arriving in Chicago in August 1945, I received a call from Mary Ann Kline, the InterVarsity office manager, trying to explain to me the SFMF Inter-Varsity merger. I was experiencing serious culture shock after five years of living in the equatorial forest of the Ubangi and had great difficulty comprehending these events.

Mary Ann said in effect, "We want to talk to you about the possibility of your helping us."

Indeed, I had been in and understood the SFMF. But, InterVarsity—in America? I knew nothing about it! Finally I agreed, with the approval of my missionary board to serve as Missions Director, pro tem. I was informed that Christy Wilson from Princeton Seminary would assume his duties as full-time missions director in January 1946.

Although I had already enrolled in a doctoral program, it seemed to me for the sake of world missions and that of the SFMF that I should make myself available to InterVarsity. In the fullness of time, Christy Wilson arrived and I thank God for his friendship and fellowship in Christ.

I intended to retire from the scene as soon as he

became established in his position. Christy, however, requested that I continue to assist him in preparing for the great Toronto International Missionary Convention, December 1946. So we worked together. He sent me to Boston to what is now Gordon-Conwell Theological Seminary and Gordon College, then a Bible and missionary training school.

I shared with the students and administration there the exciting plans for the Toronto Convention. Christy also gave me the assignment to personally invite as a speaker Dr. Harold John Ockenga to represent the "new evangelical look." Ockenga then was a young man regarded as the epitome of the new look in evangelicalism. He was the minister of Boston's prestigious Park Street Church, fearlessly proclaiming the gospel of the Lord Jesus Christ.

The "Toronto strategy" also included securing Samuel Zwemer as the representative of the Student Volunteer era. It was a beautiful thing to behold—the coming together of the plans for the Toronto Convention. As we prayed we asked, "Who will come?"

A missionary convention like that could not have been held in America at that time. A student missionary convention on an American campus in 1940-46 was unthinkable. There was no personal God, at least to the post-war academicians. Man determined his own destiny. Prayer in academia was an unknown word. But, the University of Toronto had a faculty of religion. Consequently it was more probable that a student missionary convention might be convened there.

Five hundred and seventy were enrolled at the Toronto Convention! What a thrill it was to see how God had answered prayer. From then on, continuing with 1948, the Urbana missionary conventions have been held at the University of Illinois in Urbana. Under the sovereign hand of God, the initial arrangements for Urbana were made through the faithful mediation of InterVarsity Board Chairman Herbert J. Taylor. In 1947 I returned to the Ubangi with my family for a second term. But in 1951 I was at Urbana again.

God was vindicating His Word in a new and dramatic manner in the reconstituted student missionary movement of the 1950s, '60s and '70s.

A sequence of mission directors succeeded Christy Wilson who, after a year and a half of initial leadership, left for his doctoral studies at the University of Edinburgh and subsequent service in the Middle East. Norton Sterrett, Wesley Gustafson, David Adeney and Eric Fife served as mission directors with the assistance of Lois Thiessen as interim on several occasions.

David Howard became missions director in 1967, having had extensive missionary experience in Latin America. The missionary training camp begun by David Adeney in the early 1950s was expanded by Howard to include overseas training camps in Central America. Students began developing their own regional missionary conferences during the years between the Urbana Conventions. Under John Kyle, who succeeded Howard as missions director, the Urbana attendance reached 18,000!

The development of student missionary activity in North America far exceeded the greatest expectations of the founders of the SFMF 50 years ago. Some of us in 1933-34 used to pool our modest resources, sometimes only quarters and dimes, to print a little tract entitled, "12 Outstanding Scientists Speak for God." We sent that tract to freshmen in the Big Ten universities with a copy of the *Gospel According to Saint John.* We could only afford to do one university each semester. We now observe university professors by the hundreds attending Urbana looking for ways to share the Lord Jesus Christ with the peoples of the world! As the Psalmist said, "This is the Lord's doing; It is marvelous in our eyes" (Ps. 118:23, *NASB*).

"Do nothing from selfishness or empty conceit, but with humility of mind let each of you regard one another as more important than himself" (Phil. 2:3, *NASB*). Now that's a simple command. Do not merely look out for your own personal interests, but also for the interests of others—another command. Who is this speaking and where is he? The apostle Paul wrote his message to the Philippian Christians from prison. He wrote this Epistle of "joy" to people who are free, while he is bound! Yet he is free in his spirit! Free in his imprisonment to write to people who were liberated by his ministry as a missionary. He says, "Have this attitude in yourselves which was also in Christ Jesus" (v. 5, *NASB*).

The Lord Jesus fully existed in the form of God yet did not regard equality with God as a thing to be grasped. He emptied himself taking the form of a servant. The bond servant role model of the Lord is still valid. It is observed as taking on the likeness of those whom we seek to help, identifying with them in their culture, becoming obedient to God to the point of death.

The future of the Student Foreign Missions Fellowship is directly associated with obedience in suffering. That individual or organization only looking out for its own interests and not the interests of others is doomed, including organizations like SFMF. But God has raised us up in the Lord Jesus to fulfill His purpose throughout the world. God is faithful. Jesus Christ is the same yesterday, today and forever.

9

On Being an Effective Follower
by
Paul McKaughan

Modeling is always God's way of transmitting truths. That's why the Incarnation is such a marvelous communications lesson. Christ became flesh and lived among us and we can see just how He did His redemptive work as we read the pages of the sacred Scripture.

During this conference you've been able to rub shoulders with men and women who have been following Christ for years and can say just as the apostle Paul said, "Follow our example" (see 1 Thess. 3:9). We as a generation have been robbed of our biblical models to a large degree. That's why gatherings like these are so precious.

I'd like to examine four categories of *following*. We'll take a look at the effective follower and his God, the effective follower and his own self-image, the effective follower and his team, the effective follower and his boss or colleague.

The Effective Follower and His God
Have you ever thought about the fact that we have a user mentality? And to many of us God is a very utilitarian kind

of a creature. Chuck Swindoll quotes a poem by Wilbur Rees in his book *Improving Your Serve,* in which Rees says that he'd like to buy about $3 worth of God, not enough to explode his soul or disturb his sleep, just enough to equal a cup of warm milk or a snooze in the sunshine. He doesn't want enough of God to make him love a black man or pick beets with a migrant. He wants ecstasy, not transformation. He wants warmth of the womb, not a new birth. He wants a pound of the eternal in a paper sack. He really only wants to buy $3 worth of God. [1]

Does that sound like your walk with God? I have spent so much of my devotional life looking for promises, and things that are going to make me feel good, realized and challenged. And yet we read in Deuteronomy 17: "And it shall be with him [speaking of God's Word], and he shall read it all the days of his life, that he may learn to fear the Lord his God, by carefully observing all the words of this law and these statutes" (v. 19, *NASB*).

The story is told of C.T. Studd when he was an old man in England. I believe he was at a Keswick conference, when some of the conferees got up early one morning and saw a light under Studd's door. They were concerned over his advanced age and failing health, so they knocked on his door, but no one answered. Upon opening the door to his room, they found Studd on his knees bowed over his bed. They shook him a little, then asked, "Mr. Studd, what are you doing?"

He replied, "I'm reading the Scriptures."

"What are you getting from the Lord?"

And Studd said, "I'm looking for commands to obey."

One of the reasons we have such difficulty in our own human relationships is that as we're looking through the Scriptures, we're looking for things to feed our own self-image and self-worth and we're not looking for commands to obey. If you want to be an effective follower in your relationship to God, line yourself up with God's revealed will; look for commands to obey.

Let me quote from Andrew Murray's book, *With Christ in the School of Prayer,* "When the Holy Ghost, Christ, descended into their hearts, they desired the very blessings which Christ as our high priest obtains for us by His prayer from the Father. To pray in Christ's name is therefore to be identified with Christ as to our righteousness and to be identified with Christ in our desires by the indwelling of the Holy Ghost, to pray in the Spirit, to pray according to the will of the Father."[2]

Prayer is one of the greatest means available to align ourselves up with God's will. Somehow we get the idea that our prayer life is a way to invent a future that God doesn't know anything about or has not pre-ordained. But one of the greatest values of prayer is that it lines my will up with Christ's will. I pray those prayers that I know are in His will and receive from Him in my own life and ministry those things He has promised. It's a means of obeying and believing, obeying and trusting God for those things that He wants me to gather from Him to be an effective follower.

The Effective Follower and His Self-Image

If you think right, you're going to act right, to a large degree. Now if someone said to me, Paul, what are the images that burst into your mind when somebody says, Paul McKaughan, what are you thinking? I have to tell you, *follower* is not one of them. I'd like to think Paul McKaughan—great saint, great missionary statesman, great whatever. But look at the apostle Paul as he addresses his letters. It's Paul, the bond servant of Jesus

Christ. Look at Christ as He viewed His own image, Christ the servant.

I find that my self-image is made up of a past, a present and a future. As I look at the *past*, I see some things that are very important to the making up of my self-image. I see that God created me in the image of His own son Jesus Christ. I was created in the image of the triune God. That's a marvelous thing.

I see that sin came in and I began choosing my way rather than God's way. And I was bent towards independence. In fact I became absolutely enslaved by that independent attitude so that I wanted my way—my way above all other ways, my way rather than God's way, my way rather than the way that my rulers and those in authority wanted. I wanted my way! I was condemned in my never ending pursuit of my way. And yet in my past I find that Christ died for me and Scripture says I died with Him, that I should live no more to that law of sin, the law of my own way and He freed me by His death on the cross, that in the life of Christ that's now within me I have the possibility of following God as never before. That's all part of my past.

I find in the *present*, as I look at my self-image, the tendency to want my own way is still there. But Christ has given me freedom from that law of sin and death and I now have the ability to choose to follow after Him and after those He has placed in authority over me.

For the *future* I have great hope and great encouragement because I know that the one who began that work of grace in my life is the one who is going to bring it to its completion (see Phil. 1:6). And one day I am going to be in the image of Jesus Christ, in the image of God again. I'll be a perfect follower, perfect servant of the living God.

How do I make that a reality right here and now? That's where men like Christy Wilson, former tentmaker to Afghanistan, come in; that's where the modeling comes in. It's in these lives I can see truth of the passage of Scripture that says if you humble yourself, God in His time will raise you up. I know it's a biblical truth that I'm crucified with Christ (see Gal. 2:20). And I know that the servant Christ lives within me, and the one who is obedient to the Father is down deep inside, but it's still very difficult for me to take that role of servant, to humble myself. It hurts to take the concrete opportunities that God presents to me to be a follower.

Dr. Billy Graham was over in Europe at one time holding a crusade. There was a young German evangelist who wanted to meet with him, and he wanted Dr. Graham to pray for him. Now it's very difficult at times to get to Dr. Graham. With much perseverance, this young man finally got his audience with the great Dr. Billy Graham. They talked for a bit. And then he asked Dr. Graham to pray for him, when a strange thing happened.

The two had been sitting down and all of a sudden Dr. Graham dropped down on hands and knees right in the middle of the floor and began praying for this young man. The young man didn't quite know what to do so he knelt down too. And Dr. Graham prayed that God might bless the ministry of this young German evangelist.

After they had completed the prayer, the young man, with great fear and trembling, asked Dr. Graham why he had assumed that posture in prayer. And Graham said, "As an evangelist, there are constantly people around you telling you great things about your ministry and there are all kinds of temptations to think you are more than you really are, that your ministry is more than God's grace working within you. And I find that I constantly have to remind myself of who I am before my God and before other men."

Humble yourself. What does the Scripture say? It says

that we ought to confess our sins to one another (see Jas. 5:16). Why? To forgive each other's sins? No. There is something humbling about confessing my sin to a brother and praying together for God's forgiveness. And it positions me in my own self-image in a way that God can begin to bless me. I become assertive in my following as I take that servant role in that humble position.

The Effective Follower and His Team

It's relatively easy for me to humble myself before my God. I can search the Scriptures for things to obey. And I can cultivate my mindset and say, "I want to be a servant and I'm going to do servantlike things. I'm going to hold open doors and I'm going to carry bags. And I'm going to help facilitate the ministry of others. I am truly going to be a servant." Then all of a sudden God puts us on a team with other people who don't seem to have the same kind of servant attitude that I know I ought to have.

It's important to realize that if we're born of God, we are a part of the Body. It's not voluntary. I don't select who's part of the family of God. Scripture says that God chose us before the foundation of the world (see 2 Thess. 2:13). It was done long before you even realized it. And as you become part of the Body of Christ, you get a bunch of family members that you didn't have anything to do with in choosing.

God in His sovereignty has put you next to a bunch of people in the Body because He wanted you there. Because He wanted you together to follow and become followers of the Word and assertive pursuers of His life in each other.

To that end He did some wonderful things. He gave you some gifts. Now somebody has suggested that the apostle Paul had all of the gifts. I don't believe it for a moment. I believe the great truth of the gifts is that God is distributing gifts in the Body as He wills. That says to me that I need you. And when you're ministering in the area of your gifts I have a responsibility to follow because that's God ministering to me, and I'm growing. And marvel of all marvels, you need me. One of the great things we learned in our teamwork in Brazil (we were together for about 10 years, and took about two years to learn it) was that God had His purpose in putting us together and it was good for us all.

At first we thought everything was great and this was the most marvelous bunch of saints we had ever seen. We were going to shake Brazil. After about three months we began to see all the faults. And then all we could see were the problems. We didn't understand how God could have chosen any of us. And we didn't know how God was going to use any of us. But as we worked our way through that phase we began to see Christ at work in the various members of that team, and we began to see how He was pulling us together. Finally, together we followed God within the context of the team in which He'd placed us. Some great things were going to happen.

Ed Dayton said, "Reading God's Word as though we are searching for His will for us as individuals instead of His will for us as a community can have a strange effect on our obedience. First, we often discover a sense of power-lessness. Second, we fail to talk to one another, to stir one another up to be obedient. And third, we decide somehow that we have to go it on our own. Thus we find Christians buying into plans for individual survival in a hostile world."[3]

Following God in the context of a team is a very creative experience. And I could go on for a long time about that, but I want to touch on the area of forgiveness.

C.S. Lewis says, if you can excuse something and

there was a good reason why a person did what he did, then you don't need to forgive; you just forget that. But our order from God is to forgive. And that means the person has done something really lousy; he's really stuck the knife in you. It wasn't a mistake. He really meant to do it. And it's those kinds of things—the nasty stuff—that an aggressive follower has to learn how to forgive and forget.

Somehow we have the strange idea that if we're good, we're going to reap goodness. But if you're in the Lord's service and you work with other brothers and sisters in Christ, you know that isn't true.

I've had team members say to me, "Paul, I'm gonna love 'em because I gotta love 'em. But it doesn't mean I gotta like 'em or spend time with 'em." Is that the kind of forgiveness God talks about? He says, "I forgive you and I put your sins away from Me as far as the East is from the West (see Ps. 103:12). That's the way I want you to forgive." How well do you do that?

Philippians 3 gives three steps to forgiveness. "Brethren, I do not regard myself as having laid hold of *it* yet; but one thing *I do;* forgetting what *lies* behind and reaching forward to what *lies* ahead" (v. 13, *NASB*). Aggressive following in forgiveness is one of the most difficult lessons we learn in our team relationships. And forgiveness starts when we admit we haven't yet arrived.

Paul said that he hadn't laid hold of it yet. In other words, he still needed forgiveness. But "one thing I do," he forgot what lies behind. And he did so by reaching forward to what lies ahead. I find that people are often too willing to just think about the stuff that's behind. While they're thinking about the stuff that's behind, they can't really lay hold of what's out in front, that with which God is challenging them.

One of the lessons you're going to have to learn in

Scripture is very clear: If God has placed you in a situation with someone over you, you have a responsibility to respond to that leader as you would to God."

team relationships more than any other lesson is that of forgiveness. Now, that's a tough one. It starts by keeping in mind your own fallibility and by remembering who you are and that you haven't yet arrived. It's like the parable about the man who owed much and was going to be thrown into jail. The debtor went up to the king and the king said, "I forgive you." And on the way out, the debtor found someone who owed him a little. He said, "I'm going to throw you in jail until you pay me everything you owe me" (see Matt. 18).

We're like that a lot of times. We can't seem to forgive because we can't remember that we've been forgiven. And we can't forgive because we don't have a vision that we're following after God and what He is going to do with us in the future. We're always afraid that whatever was done to us is going to derail God's plan for our lives. It can only do that if we don't let loose of past affronts and grab on to the vision for the future.

The Effective Follower and His Boss

Ministers—Presbyterian ministers especially—don't have bosses, they have colleagues. And we are always reminding ourselves that the ground is level at the foot of the cross, that I'm just as good as the next person, that we're all sinners saved by grace. We fail to remember that Romans 13:1 is even in the Bible: "Let every person be in subjection to the governing authorities. For there is no authority except from God" (RSV). I wish it said there are not *many* authorities that God has sent. But that's pretty inclusive language in the Scriptures, isn't it? There are *no* authorities except from God.

A lot of people say about themselves, my relationship to God is really great, but my relationship to the brothers—my team—is terrible. There's a lot about our relationships with people that God says mirrors our relationship to Him. If you can't love the brother whom you can see, how are you going to love God whom you can't see? If you can't respond to the authority that God has placed over you, how can you say that you're responsive to God's authority?

One of the biggest problems we have on teams all around the world, and I'm working with about 15 teams right now, is that people don't tend to like their leaders. And they think they can do a better job leading. But the problem isn't so much the leader; the problem is that we've developed a whole generation who don't think they ought to be followers. They want to be the Rockys and the Rambos of missions. But Scripture is very clear: If God has placed you in a situation with someone over you, you have a responsibility to respond to that leader as you would to God.

Watchman Nee says in his book, *Spiritual Authority*, "In order to recover authority, obedience must first be restored."[4] Many have cultivated the habit of being the head, without ever having known obedience. We must therefore learn obedience. We must let obedience be our first reaction.

Remember, modeling is always God's way. If He has chosen to give you the responsibility of leadership in the Body, what kind of a model have you set in the past? Are you an effective follower? Missionaries are normally lousy followers. We're out there ahead of the pack. We're so busy trying to carry out the Great Commission that we think God can't do without us and we don't have time to look at what He says about our relationships.

What has He called you to be? *A follower.* If you're not following in God's way in terms of relationship to Him, yourself, your team and the authority God has placed over you, then you're not being an example to the Body, an example they in turn should follow.

Project yourself 30 years down the pike in ministry. What kind of example will you be?

I've met missionaries 30 years down the pike that were still fighting for their rights. I've met missionaries down the pike who were bitter. I've met missionaries 30 years down the pike that you had to isolate because they couldn't work with anyone else. And then I've seen people like the ones here at Ben Lippen this week, people who have learned to be assertive, effective followers. Now which do you want to be?

Notes

1. Adapted from: *Improving Your Serve* by Chuck Swindoll (Waco, TX: Word, 1986).
2. Andrew Murray, *With Christ in the School of Prayer* (Grand Rapids, MI: Zondervan, 1983).
3. Ed Dayton, *Whatever Happened to Commitment* (Grand Rapids, MI: Zondervan, 1984).
4. Watchman Nee, *Spiritual Authority* (Richmond, VA: Christian Fellowship Publishers, 1972).

10

The Levites: Their Strategy and Ours

by
David Bryant

While we celebrate the one hundredth anniversary of the Student Volunteer Movement, do you know what other one hundredth anniversary we're celebrating? It began in 1886. You've heard the stories at missions conferences, I'm sure, about how Coca-Cola has penetrated almost every corner of the world. Nearly every people group of the world has access to Coca-Cola.

Yet there are 3 billion people who do not yet have access to something far more important—the gospel of our Lord Jesus Christ. So, what is it going to take to see another movement of students that stirs the church even more than in 1886 to point where our impact on the world for Christ outstrips that of Coca-Cola? A key to unlocking that may be the Levitical theme in God's thinking a long time ago.

I'd like to share a few verses from the book of Malachi, written completely to Levites and containing such exciting global perspective that even Coca-Cola would stand up and listen:

You will see it with your own eyes and say, "Great is the LORD—even beyond the borders of Israel!" (1:5).[1]

"My name will be great among the nations, from the rising to the setting of the sun. In every place incense and pure offerings will be brought to my name, because my name will be great among the nations," says the LORD Almighty (1:11).

"For I am a great king," says the LORD Almighty, "and my name is to be feared among the nations" (1:14).

"Bring the whole tithe into the storehouse, that there may be food in my house. Test me in this . . . and see if I will not throw open the floodgates of heaven and pour out so much blessing that you will not have room enough for it" (3:10).

"Then all the nations will call you blessed, for yours will be a delightful land," says the LORD Almighty (3:12).

In only four short chapters, Malachi resounds with world vision. There are other less direct statements of God's world vision here as well. And how does God propose to bring about a work whereby there are people worshipping Him and offering incense and sacrifices in every nation among every people? He gives us a clue in chapter 3:1,2:

"'See, I will send my messenger, who will prepare the way before me. Then suddenly the Lord you are seeking will come to his temple; the messen-

ger of the covenant, whom you desire, will come,'
says the LORD Almighty. But who can endure the
day of his coming? Who can stand when he
appears?"

Clearly, if you read the earlier verses of Malachi, you
will see how desperately the whole nation needed this.
But where is God going to begin?

> For he will be like a refiner's fire or a launderer's
> soap. He will sit as a refiner and purifier of silver;
> he will purify the Levites and refine them like gold
> and silver. Then the Lord will have men [all kinds
> of people] who will bring offerings in righteous-
> ness, and the offerings of Judah and Jerusalem will
> be acceptable to the Lord, as in the days gone by,
> as in former years (vv. 2-4).

So then, as the Levites are purified to fulfill their mobilizing role, which was nothing more or less than to set the
pace of a double-edged movement of worship and mission,
the people of Jerusalem and Judea, who are in desperate
need of refining and purifying, will in turn find their way
into both. They will join a movement of worship and mission to such a degree that they bring into the storehouse
all the tithes and offerings they've been withholding from
the Lord to that point.

As a result, God will pour out a blessing on His people
that will cause the nations to look up and say: "What a
blessed land. God has blessed His people." That's why
God can say in the earlier verses of Malachi 1 that beyond
the borders of Israel people will begin saying, "Great is
the Lord." Beyond the borders of Israel there will come a
movement of people who will worship Him and seek Him
and find Him.

That's the power in this theme of the Levites. The questions we're raising are: Is it time to bring back such a Levitical movement? Do we need such secret agents today for solid, revitalized missions mobilization?

I like the term *secret agents.* The Levites were carrying on their work behind the scenes. They weren't out there to get glory for themselves. It was a ministry that was God-ordained, marked by humility and done in quietness. They were servants to the work of God in the midst of His people and through His people in the midst of the nations.

All kinds of people can be Levites: goers, senders, tentmakers, those in full-time Christian ministry, those who are laymen and laywomen. And I'm offering to you the possibility that *all* of us might, in fact, as Levites, fulfill the greatest role that any of us could ever have for the cause of world evangelization.

What is it that marks a Levite? I was reading an Episcopal publication not long ago that gave some tongue-in-cheek answers to this question. In the Episcopal Church, as in some other traditions, those who shepherd the flock are called "priests." On this hypothetical nationwide survey the ideal priest is outlined.

> The perfect priest preaches exactly 12 minutes. He frequently condemns sin, but never upsets anyone. He works from 8:00 until midnight and is also a secretary. He earns $130 per week, wears good clothes, buys good books, drives a good car and gives $140 per week to the poor. He is 28 years of age and has been preaching for 30 years. He is wonderfully gentle and handsome. He gives of himself completely, but never gets too close to anyone lest he be criticized. He speaks boldly on

social issues, but never becomes politically involved. He has a burning desire to work with teenagers and spends all of his time with senior citizens. He makes 15 calls each day, visits those who are confined to their homes, ministers to the hospitalized, spends all his time evangelizing the unchurched and is always in his office when needed.

Now if your priest does not measure up, simply send a copy of this survey to six other parishes that are tired of their priest too. Then bundle up your priest and send him to the church at the top of this list. In one week you will receive back 1,643 priests. At least one of them is guaranteed to be perfect. Have faith in this chain letter. One parish broke the chain and got its old priest back in less than three months![2]

We laugh, but many of us feel trapped by our sense of God's high expectations, by which we disqualify ourselves. This need not happen. Let's review the job definition of the perfect priest as far as the Scriptures are concerned.

Levites live out their ministry in three areas: as intercessors—pray-ers—seeking God's face and making Him the focus of attention. Second, they serve as vision-givers, teaching the Word of God to the people and modeling the vision of what God's call on the nation is all about. They give all God's people a vision about how to live as priests consistently and practically, in the center of God's concern for the whole world.

The third part of their role is one of life-style. Most of the Levites were lay people. Actually, there were two classifications: priests and Levites. All the priests were Levites, but not all the Levites were priests. There was only a small segment of the total population of Levites who actually lived at any one time in Jerusalem and worked in the Temple. In fact many came in on a rotating basis though there was a way provided for those who wanted to take up full-time residence in the Temple to apply for that and to be accepted. But even then if they were at the Temple, they were there to assist those of the Levitical clan called the *Aaronic* clan, out of the tribe of Aaron.

The Aaronic Levites were what we might call the full-time spiritual workers. A few of the rest of the Levites were working in the Temple to serve them but the majority were living out among the other tribes, scattered throughout the land, carrying out their mobilization duties in all three areas of prayer, vision-giving and life-style. The majority were self-supporting to a meager degree. They would each be given a little plot of land to work and a few sheep to graze. And that's where a good deal of their food came from.

So there's an interesting mixture here. Some were full-time and others were tentmaking, or self-supporting. But in order for daily survival, both groups were dependent upon the gifts that the people of Israel brought as offerings to the Lord.

Certain portions of the offering were given to the Levites to supply their food and their clothing. The Levites, whether they were full-time professionals or self-supporting, were a constant barometer to the Israelites about what the nation's spiritual condition looked like. And that's why the Levites were identified with the poor, the lepers, the widows and the foreigners. Like those other classifications they too were very vulnerable, weak and dependent for ultimate physical survival upon the graciousness, the love and the consistent obedience of the Israelites to their God.

So if, for example, the Levites who lived in your village were suffering with degrees of poverty, it was indisputable evidence that many others were not giving heart and life to the Lord as they ought. If they did, a portion of that giving would supply the Levite's needs. They would be able to live in a proper fashion as well. That was part of their ministry in terms of life-style. They bore the sins of others, as it were, and became God's call for repentance and revival.

But whether by prayer, vision-giving or life-style, they took Israel in two directions, one toward worship and the other toward the nations. They prepared God's people to be His witnesses by leading them into renewal and then into ministry among the nations. So the SVM and the SFMF, as well as other similar student movements that we're seeing today, are in many cases re-enacting for us what the Levites were *in principle*.

Let me give you three or four illustrations of Levites at work today. Then we're going to see if the New Testament supports the fact that we ought to expect God to turn to this approach for mobilizing a new missions movement in the years just ahead.

Yesterday we had a dear friend with us, a retired missionary from India. "Aunt Edith" Morgan worked in India for 27 years and was right in on the ground floor in assisting the beginnings of an outreach called the Friends Missionary Prayer Band (FMPB). FMPB models many things that ought to be going on in missions today. It is totally indigenous and grass roots. About 30,000 lay people, for the most part in South India, are involved in over 1,500 prayer bands throughout South India. Most of these prayer bands meet every Wednesday to fast and pray most of the night.

Now then, they always pray in two directions. They pray for church revival in their various communities, and they pray for God to raise up a major missionary thrust out of the Church to the unreached peoples of India. They are compelled by a frontier mission vision. But they also offer themselves in prayer for God to call anybody out of their prayer bands He would choose to be sent by the rest of the members of a prayer band. And they offer themselves saying that if they're not the ones to be sent they will be willing to live sacrificially to send others. Most of them are living on $90 a month as it is. Still, they're willing to sacrificially give whatever it takes to send out their own. At this point in time, over 350 missionaries have been sent out by various prayer bands, while the rest of the bands are seeking God, that He would call somebody out of their midst.

A little over 20 years ago, six young men—people like Dr. Sam Kamaleson, now with World Vision—began praying, agonizing over the unevangelized condition of India. As fairly impoverished people, they recognized that they did not have in themselves any resources equal to the task before them. So the only thing they could do was to band together and cry out to God to raise up a movement of prayer that could become a sending base. They were Levites! Out of the midst of their prayer God has raised up *other* Levites, finally, thousands of them, many of which were sent off to be missionaries. But even these continued to function as Levites while they are involved in missionary work.

Or take for example the young people I met in March when I was in Tokyo. They work with Youth with a Mission (YWAM) and come from a number of different nations. I can't give you the whole story of what they're doing in Tokyo, but let me tell you the particular God-given concern they're carrying out right now. It's the kind of thing that YWAMers often come up with that the rest of us would be scared to death of if we sensed God was telling us to do something like that. But they love to hear Him speak to them on these kinds of dreams. And the dream that He's given to this team in Tokyo is to ride the train that navigates around the outside of the city on a 12-mile journey every day.

They are riding the train once a month to spend the whole day praying over the city of Tokyo, that God would penetrate that city with the gospel. But on the twelfth month something else will happen. There are many different platforms and stations along the way. What they want to do is mobilize Christians in each part of the city to meet them on the platform in their area so when the train stops on that particular day the prayer meeting will not be inside the train, but outside in a prayer rally on the platform while the train is waiting. By the end of their day of travel on the twelfth month, they will have in fact mobilized many of the Christians in Tokyo to united, prayerful concern for their city.

Let me tell you about Wheaton College today. There are 500 students meeting weekly there in what's called the World Christian Fellowship. Do you know why? Because of a group of five Levites back in 1980. One of those Levites transferred from a secular university onto that campus. His name is David. He's now working in the Muslim world.

When David moved to that campus to get missionary training, he was burdened with the general lack of mission vision he found there. Finally, he uncovered four other students with the same burden. They met frequently, thought and prayed, but saw no way forward apart from prayer. And so they set up a little strategy they called the "Jericho Walks." Each day they walked around each dorm of the campus praying that God would raise up mission prayer and study groups on every floor of every dorm on Wheaton campus. And they did that through the winter months; they were out there in the rain, snow and cold every day.

By that spring, God had given mission prayer and study groups to almost all of Wheaton campus! That gave a whole new birth to World Christian Fellowship, the SFMF group there in 1980. One of the characteristics of WCF from that time forth has been the prayer movement that it mobilizes on the campus. God is answering prayers so much that it seems almost unbelievable. And it's because of Levites on that campus just a few short years ago.

I believe it's time to bring back the Levites with stronger force than we've yet seen. Don't these few illustrations whet your appetite? Surely as we come to the end of the Old Testament, especially to the books of Malachi, Haggai and Zechariah, we're given the sense that God has in mind to develop something more with this principle of the Levites. For example, in Jeremiah 33:3 He says, "Call to Me, and I will answer you, and I will tell you great and mighty things, which you do not know." He describes a city that is so rejuvenated, revitalized and renewed that it becomes a praise and a glory and an honor to Him before the whole earth. At the end of that vision we're told that the city will be so full of Levites that they will not be able to be numbered—Levites everywhere!

In the last six chapters of Ezekiel we see a renewed city, a renewed Temple and a throne set up in the holy of holies. Out of the midst of the throne proceeds a flowing river giving life to the nations. How did this happen? One of the primary explanations given to Ezekiel is the work of the Levites out of the tribe of Zadok who continue to minister in the midst of all the other activity of renewal and mission.

Again in Malachi, we have a promise that there will come a day when the Lord will appear in His Temple. And the first thing He's going to do is get down to business with the Levites so that the rest of the mission might carry forward. The interesting thing is that about 400 years later, after Malachi's words, onto the scene walks a Levite by the name of John the Baptist, of the tribe of Levi. His father serves in the Temple. It's a Levite who's out in the wilderness calling God's people to prepare, because it's about time for all flesh to see the glory of God.

So, Jesus came; He followed a number of existing attempts to bring renewal to the life of Israel, all of which patterned themselves from the Levites. There was the Dead Sea community, the Kumron community, the Zealots from which the disciple James came, the Sadducees and the Pharisees. In fact, the Sadducees took their name from the Levitical clan of Zadok. They were Sadducians or the Zadokians. They believed that they were the fulfillment of Ezekiel's vision of what the Zadokian Levites were supposed to do.

In the end, however, Jesus was crucified as the result of the ruling of a council of Levites—the Sanhedrin. Which only goes to say that though the New Testament opens with a Levite in the wilderness, his real message is this: There's something better on the horizon; prepare. The renewal movements patterned after the Levites simply reinforce his conclusion. The cross shows us how deficient they all were. Something better *is* ahead.

In the book of Hebrews, over and over again the writer says that there is something better; there is a hope of renewal and mission God has put before us, because we have a priest who is a better priest. He's after the order of

168 Finishing the Task

Melchizedek. He rules not by lineage, but by the power and the authority of an indestructible life (see Heb. 7).

Jesus is a better high priest in a number of ways. Call to mind in Mark 11 when He walks into the Temple as the *real* high priest to cleanse the Temple so that it can become a place of prayer for all nations. What did He want? Not that the Temple was to become a prayer group for the Chinese world or something similar. No, He wanted the Temple to become the center of worship, without any obstruction so that all kinds of nations could find their way into the presence of the living God.

That's the kind of better high priest we've been given. He brings whole nations and people with Him! And we have a better temple. Take just one illustration in Revelation 1. When Jesus describes the churches as lampstands, He's taking that right out of the imagery of the Temple, the candles in the holy place. And when you see Jesus clothed in Revelation 1, He's wearing the garments of a royal priest. He's moving among the churches in the holy place.

When we think about church planting, what are we doing? We're raising up more lampstands in the temple in which Jesus is surveying. He wants to have His temple populated with lampstands from every people, tribe and nation so that He can fulfill His priesthood to the fullest in a temple that encompasses the whole earth.

I like what it says in 1 John 2:2: "He is the atoning sacrifice for our sins, and not only for ours but also for the sins of the whole world." There's a whole new understanding of the sacrificial system, not only in that it is fulfilled in the person of God's own Son, but that it clearly breaks open God's redemptive work for the whole world. We have a better *sacrifice*.

We also have a better priestly movement. In fact, Revelation 1 tells us that we have been redeemed by the blood of Christ and made into kings and priests. Revelation 5 says worthy is the lamb who has redeemed us from every tongue and tribe and nation and made us into kings and priests (see vv. 9,10). And if you study the throne room scene in Revelation 4 and 5, it is a mixture of throne room and temple. That is the imagery that John sees there. Even the elders are wearing crowns and yet holding incensers. They are kings, but they are priests too. When they fall down and place the incensers before the Lamb, what's in those incensers? It's the prayers of all the saints. So there's a mobilization of the whole people of God into a people of prayer.

In fact when you flash back to Acts 1, you discover something curious: Jesus' strategy for world evangelization. He left behind only one strategy, which was to "wait," stay put and keep hanging around. In other words, wait on *God's* initiative. And that means, quite simply, *pray*—be Levites.

Now this was very active waiting. It wasn't passive doodling until God made a move. They were out in the market place, in the Temple, praying and moving about. They were holding committee meetings too. But it's different from how most of us do it.

We hold committee meetings and lay out plans and then have a prayer meeting that God will bless our plans. But they had a prayer meeting that filled them with such a sense of hope of what God was about to do that they finally said: "You know we had better have a committee meeting to get a few things organized because God's about to answer in powerful ways and we need to be ready to move with Him."

Yes, He left behind one strategy—a prayer movement. Acts 2 says that the Church's hallmark was that they were continually in prayer. In Acts 4, when they first began to meet persecution, they came together as a band of people in prayer. Like Levites, John and Peter called them together to seek in prayer the Lord's power for witnessing. And it moves that way all the way through Acts till we come to chapter 13, where you have interestingly enough, the various gifts of Ephesians 4—apostles, prophets and teachers—three of the five major gifts that Paul refers to in Ephesians. And what are they doing? They're ministering to the Lord. They're waiting, they're watching, they're listening, they're fasting, they're laying aside other concerns.

Here are the Levites who have been giving vision; by their very gifts they are vision-givers. They are also people of intercession. And even their life-style is characterized by vulnerability (fasting) within their ministry on behalf of that whole church in Antioch. When God speaks, what does He do? He calls two of those Levites to be sent out of the five. The other three are left behind—not just to send them, but to bring the whole church into the sending process so that when Paul and Barnabas finish their missionary journey they can return to a whole church of pray-ers ready to listen and praise God for their report.

Throughout the New Testament expansion on the Levitical movement the original missions mobilization strategy of this Old Testament theme remains intact, at least in principle. In very simple terms, it is summarized in one phrase: *in the midst.* Levites were always in the midst of things. This was how they mobilized God's people: Just as the whole nation was a base of operations for God's Kingdom in the midst of the unreached peoples around them, so the Levites carried out their calling— intercession, vision-giving, modeling in life-style—*in the midst* of the Israelites, being in embryo form for them what they, in turn, were to become for the nations of the earth.

Paul, when he describes his own "great commission" in Colossians 1:23—2:3 talks about life-style. He's filling up what's lacking in the sufferings of Christ. He's laboring and struggling with God's energy in him. But it is a labor—that's life-style. His life-style is very characteristic of someone who identifies with the poor, the broken and the suffering. In terms of *vision-giving,* he's making the Word of God fully known. He's teaching and admonishing every person so that he may present every person complete in Christ. He's helping the Church to understand, he says, the mystery of Christ, which is nothing less than God's redemptive plan for the whole earth. He's a vision-giver.

Third, Paul is a man of prayer. In fact, he says in the opening verses in chapter 2 that he struggles and labors even for those who have never seen his face.

Paul is obviously a Levite. In principle, he displays the three characteristics: life-style, vision-giving and intercession. This is his "great commission," fulfilled at times in the missionary mode, but still, forever, the Levite. And what is Paul's ultimate burden in this mobilization process? He gives it in Colossians 1:27, that in the midst of the nations, the Church might understand that Jesus who's in the midst of them is "the hope of glory." I like to paraphrase it this way: Christ—the assurance of all the glorious things that God has in store for the universe.

Of course, we must thrust out our laborers. We need tens of thousands more. But Paul's mobilization strategy took the role of a Levite. He knew that the Church, wherever it's to be found, in Colossae or wherever, has in the midst of it a High Priest who's developing that church into a temple even as Paul describes in 1 Corinthians 3. And those temples thrive and grow in the midst of unreached peoples—the nations. But unless these temples—the Church—know who Jesus is in the midst of them, the Church can never be the witness it must be. Often, the "hidden people" of whom we speak (3 billion out of reach of the gospel) exist because of the hidden person. Christ is hidden to the missionary people He has called to reveal His salvation to the whole world. On the other hand, once they do know Him, then God will see to it that by one means or another the nations will become an audience of what God is doing in the midst of His own people, moving unbelievers to a saving faith that calls them into the temple with them. Then, the unreached themselves become immediate prospects for a Levitical-style outreach.

The Church's evangelistic enterprise is, in fact, full of priestly images. Let me take one of them, Romans 15. Paul provides a whole new understanding of what missionary service is and how it fits into the Levitical dimension of missions. And throughout the whole Epistle of Romans, Paul is functioning as a Levite on behalf of the church in Rome, mobilizing it to increasingly develop into a church whose faith is heard throughout the whole earth. Paul says, "I have written you quite boldly on some points, as if to remind you of them again, because of the grace God gave me to be a minister of Christ Jesus to the Gentiles with the priestly duty of proclaiming the gospel of God, so that the Gentiles might become an offering acceptable to God, sanctified by the Holy Spirit. Therefore I glory in Christ Jesus in my service to God" (Rom. 15:15-17, *NIV*). What kind of service?

It's a priestly service. "I will not venture to speak of anything except what Christ has accomplished through me in leading the Gentiles to obey God by what I have said and done—by the power of signs and miracles, through the power of the Spirit. So from Jerusalem all the way around to Illyricum, I have fully proclaimed the gospel of Christ. It has always been my ambition to preach the gospel where Christ was not known, so that I would not be building on someone else's foundation" (vv. 18-20).

His is a priestly ambition. He wants to be able to offer onto the altar of God new offerings that have never been placed there before. But these offerings are the lives of people from among the nations who previously had never seen or heard. Paul's priestly ministry is first to the church in Rome, which he hopes will eventually send him on to Spain, as he says in the latter part of chapter 15. That's part of why he's ministering to them as a Levite, that they'll send him on to the unreached. Not only is his ministry to the Christian community to bring it into the fullness of Christ, but also as he himself is launched on into pioneer missionary work he sees missions as a priestly duty to the unreached on behalf of the whole people of God.

So, is it time to bring back the Levites? Of course the priesthood of believers remains a given. We're not arguing with that. Still it seems that "way-makers" (which the apostles were, for example) have always retained a vital role both on the inward and the outward journey. Sometimes the priesthood of believers is interpreted in our culture to mean, "I can take care of my own spiritual life, thank you very much. I'm my own priest and responsible for my own spiritual growth."

According to 1 Peter 2, however, this priesthood is corporate and for the purpose of declaring the marvelous works of God before a world of darkness. So maybe there *is* a time in certain generations when God needs to raise up a Levitical movement inside the Church-at-large to pattern and model what the whole priesthood of believers is about. Clearly, this is often God's strategy to bring us all back to our priesthood role in the direction God intended,

Levites will always be needed as long as . . . there are seekers after God who need to be led, both within the people of God and among those who are being touched by the missionary witness of His people."

first in worship and then in mission to the very ends of the earth.

Most major missions movements have involved five phases as seen in all these examples: (1) movements of prayer, which (2) renews the vision of Christ—that Colossians 1:27, (3) leading to unity and resolve in the church to get on with the work of Christ together, (4) revitalizing current ministries and (5) expanding the work of the Kingdom where Christ has not been known before among the unreached. If that pattern is a valid one, then Levites have to be somewhere right at the beginning because it is such people, in principle, who will launch a movement of prayer.

Levites will always be needed as long as: (1) Christ in the midst of His people is our strategy—with that then being proclaimed to the whole world; (2) temple building is our objective—that is, church planting; (3) there are seekers after God who need to be led, both within the people of God and among those who are being touched by the missionary witness of His people; (4) the Church struggles with periods of paralysis and blindness, failing to be the missionary people God has called us to be.

Furthermore, Levites are needed *today* because we face 3 billion unreached people among whom as many as 6 million new churches must be planted. In addition, we face major unpenetrated worldviews. One of the major victories to be won when confronting the Islamic and Hindu worlds, for example, will be when they see Christians who know God so vitally and love Him so wholeheartedly that they are compelled to find out more. That requires a missionary team living out its life together as Levites. Then, Levites are required today because we face urban centers in desperate need of a united church, united above all as a praying church.

Dr. Raymond Bakke has conducted consultations on

evangelism in 100 urban centers around the world. Leaders in those urban centers, discussing what it will take to penetrate their city with the gospel, found at least two interesting discoveries. First, about eight of the ten major barriers to the penetration of the gospel in the cities of our world are *internal,* not external—the problems are within the life of the church in those cities. Second, one of the greatest pleas Bakke heard from leaders was this: We need to get together in prayer.

When I finished consultations on united prayer in just seven Asian cities in March, I came away absolutely certain that not only are certain leaders pleading for this, but they are ready as never before to be involved together if only someone will show them the way.

In Singapore we'd had a consultation of 60 leaders that ran four hours. Then we got down on our knees for 10 minutes of silence just to listen and see if God was saying anything to us about where He wanted this work to go. A young man about 28 years of age just completing his preparation for missionary service stood up. If you know Chinese culture you realize it was a courageous thing for a young person to stand up among his elders and testify to any kind of vision or dream or to offer strong initiative. But he stood up with all the graciousness of Chinese culture, apologizing to his elders and yet saying that God had told him during the 10 minutes to have courage and say what he had to say.

He began to share with us a vision God had given him two and a half years ago, while he was at the beginning of missionary preparation. God wanted him to help raise up a united prayer movement in that city. And the number he said God had given to him was 2,000 Christians gathered unitedly and regularly in prayer for spiritual awakening and world evangelization. Then he turned to his elders, and in a perfect Levitical way he said, "I graduate at the end of this spring. But, I would be willing to work with any of you to give myself for the next three months in any way you'd like to use me that would in any fashion help to enhance such a movement of prayer, if that's what you would choose." That's the role of a Levite.

Any of us have the capacity to do the same in our churches and with leadership in our campus groups. Furthermore, if we bring God's people together into such a movement of prayer, we have the perfect environment to build a world vision, to create a climate where the voice of God can be heard, whether He calls to go or to send, and to create a sending base, a launching pad for those who are to be sent. It is the perfect approach to all three needs. We *must* revive the Levitical movement.

Are we at the threshold? Yes. And one illustration of this is in our world of youth, which involves Youth for Christ International. Two and a half years ago in a period of tremendous organizational crisis, their World Leadership Team, meeting in Hong Kong, got down on their faces and cried out to God for an answer to some of their dilemmas. And they sensed God speaking to them. There, in prayer, these leaders among high school students in some 95 nations of the world sensed collectively that God was calling them to be Levites.

Collectively, they came to the conclusion that God was saying, "I will deliver you from your dilemmas if you will be willing to serve me in raising up a Worldwide Youth Prayer Movement (and this is the exact phrase God gave them). The leaders shared this vision with their international board of directors. For half a day they discussed the unreached youth of the world, what they termed *One Young Billion*. The second half of the day was spent sharing vision for how to go about raising the youth prayer movement that would depend not upon polished material and high-powered programming, but upon dissemination of itself, sweeping from one young life to another.

Today God has given us a very simple strategy for mission mobilization. First, you begin to live a life that shows that you identify with God's heart for the whole world. Then you start giving a vision every chance you get of God's heart for the world, and how that is all fulfilled through the person of Jesus, who dwells in all of His glory in the midst of us. Third, you look for those, even a handful at the beginning, who would be willing to gather with you to seek the face of God for both the inward and outward journey, for spiritual awakening and for evangelization of the world.

Notes

1. Scripture quotations in this chapter are taken from the *New International Version.*
2. Source unknown.

11

Seven Sources of Weariness in the Ministry
by
Gordon MacDonald

A year or two ago there was a lot of publicity and hype over a particular boxing match. Sugar Ray Leonard, an Olympic Gold Medalist, then welterweight champion, was coming out of retirement. He had quit boxing a couple of years earlier after suffering a detached retina.

But Leonard decided to come back and give it one more shot. Even the most apathetic among us couldn't disguise a bit of interest in how Leonard would fare.

The next morning in the Boston newspaper, there was a huge picture, about 6 columns wide, of Sugar Ray Leonard sitting in a corner of the ring with a very glazed look in his eyes. Reporters asked him what was on his mind as he sat there after winning the fight. All Sugar Ray said was, "It's over."

I thought back to how many men and women of God I've known who, having generated enthusiasm, ambition and idealism in their walk with the Lord have been knocked squarely on their backsides, and have looked up through the fog and said, "It's over."

Many of us have read biographies of some of the great spiritual warriors of the past. While some of these books are excellent, others are oversentimentalized. They make their subjects out to be unbeatable people who never suffered from fatigue, fear or burnout. Be aware of this, and don't get bogged down in trying to live out the glamorous and unrealistic portraits some of these books paint. At one time or another, possibly many times, these saints sat in a corner and muttered, "From where I sit, it's all over."

I've had that feeling on a number of occasions and have talked with many men and women in the ministry who have also. I always use a particular passage of Scripture when I run into these "It's-all-over" situations in myself or in others. It's Psalm 63:1, a passage written by a man who, at least for the moment, believes the end is at hand.

There is some disagreement as to the context of this Psalm. Some feel it was written during David's early adulthood when he was being chased around in the wilderness by Saul. I'm of the school who feel it was written while David was being kicked out of Jerusalem, as the result of a rebellion led by his son Absalom.

Either one of these contexts would suffice, however, because in both cases David is knocked flat. I'm going to spend half this message dealing with the first verse of the Psalm and the second half on the remainder of the passage. I know that isn't good biblical exegesis, but that's okay.

> O God, thou art my God,
> I seek thee, my soul thirsts
> for thee; my flesh faints for thee, as in a dry and
> weary land where no water is *(RSV)*.

This verse suggests exhaustion and weariness, someone whose reserves are so low he can barely think.

What are some sources of weariness in ministry? Let me offer five possible examples.

First, we see a man who's drained, tapped out. I know what that drained feeling is like; I was a pastor for nearly 25 years. Almost every Monday morning, without fail, I woke up with little or no energy. When you preach anywhere between two and four times on a Sunday, week after week, for years on end, something's got to give. Add to that all the hands you have to shake and all the smiles you have to smile, even at people you don't like. In addition, there are people with real needs, who come at you day after day—relentlessly.

I'm not speaking of an out of the ordinary situation here. This is reality. I simply can't go on day after day at top speed without being drained. So Monday morning after Monday morning, I would wake up numb with fatigue.

A second type of fatigue is contained in the words *dried out*. That takes place when the amount you give grossly exceeds what you're taking in. When that happens we tend to stay away from the disciplines of the Spirit—to the point that our own inner being becomes incapable of flexing and adjusting to the realities all around us.

This kind of fatigue has happened to me many times. I forget to keep myself spiritually fit and suddenly I arrive at a point where I'm incapable of giving anymore. I get irritable and angry and all I want to do is escape.

In Psalm 63, David is probably in a dried-out condition for the entire year after his sin with Bathsheba. He's so drained spiritually that he doesn't even know what the prophet Nathan is talking about during their confrontation.

Let me give you a third source of fatigue. I call it *the distorted condition*. We get so barraged by external input and impulses that we begin to lose sight of the central truths of our lives.

"Buy this, join that, give to my charity, join this organization, give your money to my cause." We're so bombarded with noise from the so-called experts, the celebrities, the athletes and the beauty queens that we lose track of the still, small voice we should really be listening to.

Another point of weariness is what I call *the devastated condition*. In Scripture we can see this clearly in the apostle Paul. In 2 Corinthians 1, he says, "We faced such pressure that we came to a moment when we despaired of life itself" (see v. 8). The intense persecution left him feeling that he had to run, and the best place to run was to death itself. There are more than a few men and women in ministry who've wanted to escape so badly that they've said on occasion, "I'd prefer dying to this."

There is also *the disillusioned condition*. This begins to take place when it suddenly feels as though all our ideals have gone askew.

Moses experienced disillusionment. At the age of 40 he finally wakes up to what's going on with the Hebrew people, his own flesh and blood. When he discovers an Egyptian beating on a Hebrew slave, he thinks he's found his chance, so he kills the Egyptian.

Not only do the Egyptians frown on this, but even his own people don't think he's a hero. So he runs to the desert out of fear, but also, I think, out of disillusionment. He took his best shot and failed.

William Booth, the founder of the Salvation Army, also experienced disillusionment. He and his wife Catherine almost single-handedly started a new effort to reach broken people in the slums of England—an effort that ultimately took hold around the world.

But Booth came to a point of utter disillusionment. He

*T*here are times in the life
of any woman or man, no
matter how old or experienced
they are, when they need to
know that God's strong right
hand is upholding them."

wanted to quit. Here is a portion of a letter he wrote to his wife: "I wonder whether I couldn't get something to do in London, some kind of respectable secretaryship that would keep us going. I know how difficult things are to obtain without friends or influence, as I am now fixed. But we must hope against hope, I suppose."[1]

Being disheartened also brings on weariness. When I was a young pastor in New England, I was intimidated when I drove down one of the main thoroughfares into the city of Boston. I looked to my left across the river and saw the spires of Harvard; further on down the road I saw the buildings of MIT (Massachusetts Institute of Technology); still further on I saw the towers of the multinational corporations that dotted the Boston skyline. I'd often say to myself, "Can I make any difference at all in this world?"

You can't go to the mission field, pastorate or into any ministry endeavor without being disheartened by surface things, or the seeming vastness of your task.

When I was in high school and college I ran on the track teams. I learned quickly that a successful athlete will do a lot of studying on the sources of fatigue. You can't run a Boston Marathon, for example, without knowing how to physically and emotionally cope with the fatigue and pain that's going to hit you around the seventeenth or eighteenth mile.

How do you cope with these sources of weariness? There are four environments reflected in Psalm 63, beginning with verse two and the word *sanctuary*. In verse 6, you can see the second environment—the *nightroom*, or the bedroom. The sanctuary, in the language of the hunter, is a safe harbor for birds and animals. It's a place where they can live and grow in security. The nightroom is a place of escape. A place where we can be alone with our deepest thoughts and longings and not be disturbed.

In verse 7, there is a third environment—*the shadow of thy wings.* In Deuteronomy 32:11, Moses writes a beautiful message to Israel. He talks about the bird of the desert who tries its wings, the eagle that nudges the eaglet out of the nest and allows it to free-fall off the cliff. It's a rather dramatic way to teach young birds to fly, but the mother and father are always there to make sure no harm comes to their offspring.

Jesus also seizes the same metaphor as He looks over the city of Jerusalem. In grief and tears he says, "How often would I have gathered your children together as a hen gathers her brood under her wings, and you would not!" (Luke 13:34, *RSV*).

The fourth environment, if I have studied it properly, is *the strong hand of the father* to a child who is losing his balance.

One of the most vivid memories I have of my father was the day he taught me to ski. When we got to the top, my father picked me up and placed me between his legs and his skis. He said, "I want you to feel how I turn, how I move. Each time you feel me doing something, you do exactly the same thing."

Then there came that magic moment when I felt him shove me gently ahead and say, "Go ahead, son, you're on your own." If he saw me losing my balance he quickly caught up with me, put his hands on my shoulders and drew me back to his body.

There are times in the life of any woman or man, no matter how old or experienced they are, when they need to know that God's strong right hand is upholding them.

In Psalm 63:1, David says, "O God, thou art my God, . . . my soul thirsts for thee" (*RSV*). I am impressed that this Psalm does not reflect a David who is seeking revenge. This is a Psalm that speaks to the number one issue every man or woman must pursue in these kinds of conditions.

Whenever you start a new game of pool or billiards, someone gets a triangular rack and puts all the balls back into place. They turn to the person with the cue and the cue ball and say, "You break."

That is a picture of everyday life for someone in the ministry. We go out every morning, as it were, perfectly formed in Christlikeness, at least by intention or ideal. Then someone in the world says, "Break." And the cue ball comes at us—the ball of events and competitors and problems and fears and anxieties that seem to have no rationale. Before many hours have gone by, our day is fragmented. So we take out the rack, put everything together and start over again.

That's what David is doing—he knows he's been blown apart by events, most of which he has no control over, and he says, "Oh, God, I enter the sanctuary and behold your power and glory. Bring my soul back into shape again. I relax in the strength of your strong right hand; help me retain my balance."

That's what all of us in the ministry need to learn—that we can rest and lean on the Father for support. Even though we're sitting in the corner, knocked for a loop, staring through glazed eyes, none of us ever has to say, "It's all over."

Note

1. Harold Bigby, *The Life of William Booth* (New York: Macmillan, 1920).

12

A Short-term Mission with a Long-term Vision

by
Jayson D. Kyle

A few short years ago, two soccer teams were competing;
Brazil and Argentina. With two minutes to go in the game,
the score was tied one to one and the crowd was in a
frenzy. Brazil got the ball and moved it downfield. A Brazilian player took a shot in front of the goal, but it went wide.
Everyone was sure the game was going to end in a tie.

But a penalty occurred just outside the goalie box. And
as Argentina's players lined up their defense barrier, the
crowd of 250,000 quieted to a whisper. It was only 30 sec-
onds to the end of the game. A Brazilian player leaned forward, hesitated for a moment, making his final decision
about which direction he would kick the ball. Then he
moved forward rapidly and kicked the ball toward the top
right corner of the goal. Everyone knew as soon as he
struck the ball it was going to hit the last player at the end
of the human defense barrier. For an instant the last
defense player remained rigid, watching the ball coming
directly toward him. At the last moment, he fell on his
face; the ball went over his head and into the corner of the
goal. The game ended: Brazil 2, Argentina 1.

The crowd was silent. They could not believe that an Argentina player would betray his team in the world cup. All of a sudden the player leaped up off the ground and the fans, recognizing the uniform, began to cheer. It was a Brazilian player who had lined up with the Argentine defense. He had won the game. He was a man who was in the right place at the right time and knew exactly what to do.

That is short-term missions today. I believe that today's young people, young adults and older folks, are more aware than ever of what God is doing universally and what He's doing in their lives. And they want to take part in world missions. But a lot of them are not sure they are supposed to go as career missionaries into another culture at this point.

In 1981 I had the privilege to be at the celebration of the Haystack Prayer Meeting. I remember sitting down for lunch with two university students from Chattanooga, Tennessee. Eric Pop and Wayne Newsome began to corner me with difficult questions on the pros and cons of short-term missions. At the time I had only been a mission administrator for about two years, so I struggled through each answer. Eric and Wayne were members of their InterVarsity Christian Fellowship at the University of Tennessee and were seeking God's will for their lives. Eric was president of his InterVarsity chapter and a senior, finishing in mechanical engineering. Wayne was looking forward to work in the business world.

Eric and Wayne had come to celebrate an historic prayer meeting; at the same time they were seeking to understand short-term missions. We discussed questions like: why go overseas for two years, rather than for one year? They both explained it would be much easier for them to go for one year so they wouldn't be out of the work force very long. A two-year assignment requires a three-year commitment in order to raise finances, attend cross-cultural training and work in the field. Out loud they wondered, what if God did not lead them into long-term missions after the three years? Could they trust God to help them re-enter the competitive work force after being gone for two years?

Next, they asked what training short-term missionaries received. I explained that in our Servants In Missions Abroad Program we were using the Agape International Training with Campus Crusade in Los Angeles, which called for almost a 3-month training period. They pointed out that was much longer than any other mission they had talked with. Why so long, they asked. Because I am only committed to sending people out that I know will survive, that have a ministry where they go, and then return to the states ready to make decisions about the next step God has for them was my answer.

After we finished our discussion, I felt sure I would never see those two fellows again. But a few months later, in January 1982, both Eric and Wayne applied for a two-year assignment. We assigned them to work with the Language Institute for Evangelism. By the end of the summer of '82, they had finished their cross-cultural training, and raised all their money in two weeks—incredible, but God does wonderful things when we step out in faith. I smile today when I think of their youthful faith.

Eric and Wayne spent two and a half years in Japan teaching English as a second language. Both of them had the privilege of seeing a number of people come to Jesus Christ, who are now baptized and in the church. Before they came back to the United States, they said they were both stopping by Israel to take a course in biblical theology. Today the young men are completing their studies at

Reformed Theological Seminary in Jackson, Mississippi, preparing to be church planters in Japan. Yes, I answered a few questions, but God *directed,* and Eric and Wayne *obeyed.*

Now this is not an isolated case. This is going on among thousands of men and women around the United States. I can believe that from my own experience and the experience of many others, which leads me to the premise: *The majority of tomorrow's missionaries and mission leaders will come from the ranks of those who have served as short-term missionaries.* In addressing this premise I would like to answer three questions: First, why do I believe this to be true? Second, how is a short-term missionary best prepared to take a step into a long-term mission commitment? Third, what is our responsibility to them?

I would like to just mention at this point that I'm very humbled to refer to this subject. I have had the privilege during the last eight years to be associated with many men and women who have educated me in the area of short-term missions. Some of my teachers were Bill Goheen of InterVarsity Christian Fellowship, David Hicks of Operation Mobilization and Jim Rogers of Youth with a Mission.

This fall these friends and many other mission leaders met for the fifth year to discuss the topic of short-term missions. For five days each year we struggled with such topics as: How can God move short-term missionaries to a long-term missions commitment, not just overseas but also in this country?

In many ways I feel like I am turning my back on these leaders by going to Mexico City as a church planting missionary at this time. But I have already been told that within the next couple of years we will be expected to take 30 or 40 summer missionaries in Mexico City! So I am

Face-to-face, short-term missionaries are seeing the great needs of the world today."

sure I will still be involved. I am committed to these people. And I want you to know the things I share, they would also share.

First, why do I believe it's true that short-term missionaries will produce our future long-term missionaries? History reveals some of the answers. I began looking into the past some years ago. I love history.

Let us reflect on the people who came out of World War II. Many of our missionaries on the field were not Christians during the war. My father, John Kyle, is an example of this. But he and many others saw that people had great needs. Many of them came to know Christ, returned and entered seminaries and Bible colleges, such as Wheaton and Columbia Bible College. There they came face-to-face with other students and young adults preparing to be missionaries. As a result, thousands of missionaries went out after World War II to share the gospel of Jesus Christ.

I might also point out that those returning servicemen had a direct effect on the students in the states, both on campuses and in churches. Face-to-face they had seen the great needs of the world. And face-to-face, short-term missionaries are seeing the great needs of the world today.

Briefly I would like to refer to my own experience, because it is very much a part of today's short-term mission movement. Short-term missions now is very closely linked to the Student Foreign Missions Fellowship. The last 20 years has seen a great influx of short-term missionaries into the world. It is unprecedented at any other time of history.

In the late '60s I was part of a confused generation, still struggling through a lot of values and idealism. It was during those years that short-term missionaries started to go out. I went to college and though I had a heart for missions, having returned from overseas as a missionary kid, I was not really committed to return to the field myself. I had plans to make a lot of money and *send out* missionaries. I thought that would kind of salve my conscience.

During those years, however, God began to work in my life. My future wife asked me this probing question after I had shared with her how I was going to make a million dollars: Would you be willing to pump gas for the rest of your life? The problem was, I was not, and I told her so. The other problem was that she was preparing to be a missionary nurse. You know what I thought? *What a waste of talent and beauty.* As a result of that attitude, my life began to take some hard knocks.

By my senior year of college, 40 students and I had organized a new Student Foreign Missions Fellowship at Belhaven College. It was not that we were great people. We had just begun to realize that God really wanted to use us. He did not need *us* so much, but His plan was to use men and women. So we organized our chapter and invited missionaries to speak to us. It was amazing how many missionaries we had. Today there are scores of people who are overseas as a result of those times of listening to missionaries and praying in the early morning hours. We often prayed that God would direct us to know His place for us. We sent many short-term missionaries out during those years.

I went on to seminary to receive some further Bible training, still not wanting to be a minister or a missionary. So God had a lot of work to do. During seminary I met and became a good friend of Randy Pope, a fellow student also interested in missions. Today Randy is a pastor in Atlanta, Georgia and God has enabled him to start four churches, which are all missions-minded.

Randy and another student, Mike Quarles, and I felt that we should start student conferences on world evangelization. Our conferences had speakers such as Warren Webster, Ralph Winter, Frank Barker and many others. Held in the country, our first conference was rustic. Our meetings were in a barn with a sawdust floor and backless benches. Portable johns and tents dotted the hillsides. But we were intense and committed to our task. We had 250 students from 10 states. For five years those conferences continued in southeastern United States and were used of God in many lives to raise afresh the banner of world missions. My history is very tied in with the Student Foreign Missions Fellowship.

My life is also tied in with the Student Volunteer Movement. As a high school student, I read about the life of Bill Borden and since then have read it many times. Bill died in Cairo, Egypt in 1925 at the age of 25. Earlier, Bill, at his father's death, became an instant millionaire. Yet he committed himself to work with Muslims in China. I remember saying, "If that guy can do that, I can at least commit myself to do whatever God wants me to do." Later, my wife and I went as short-term missionaries to Papua New Guinea with Wycliffe Bible Translators.

Some may say, "Well, why didn't you make a commitment for long-term missions?" I *had* committed myself to long-term missions, but I just didn't know where I fit in. I would say over 90 percent of the people that go into short-term missions, particularly those who are in college or a little bit older, have already committed themselves to missions and to do whatever God says. They just don't know exactly where they fit into the picture. And it was in Papua that we began to serve Him. Then God brought us back here to the States.

My wife and I have poured our lives into short-term

missionaries for the last eight years. I can't tell you how many hours we have spent talking with young people. My wife has put up with hundreds of phone calls during our dinner hour and late at night. But we believe in short-term missions. And I'm not the only one. I have had many comrades, both men and women, doing the same work I have been doing. They are doing it right now, because they believe that, God willing, short-termers will be the great missionary force of the future.

I believe God has been making tremendous investments in people and money over the last several years in order to prepare tomorrow's mission force. Let me give you some statistics. In 1966 we know that 600 short-term missionaries went overseas. By 1975, 5,764 were on the field. By 1984, there were 28,213. In 1986, over 30,000. And by the year 1990 over 42,000 young people, young adults and older adults will be serving overseas as short-term missionaries.

If you look at the last 10 years, at least 223,000 people have gone out from North America alone to serve as short-term missionaries. In the next 6 years, by 1992 I predict some additional 243,000 young people and adults will go overseas as short-term missionaries.

What does all this mean? For one thing it means a lot of money. It costs to put these people out on the field. Some go for two weeks and others for two and a half years. Sometimes it costs $30,000 to put a person out for two and a half years. Let's say it costs $1,500 for each short-term person. In this case, $335 million was spent on short-term missions in the last 10 years. This year alone we are talking about $50 million dollars to send out short-term missionaries. And this does not include, by the way, people who have gone out directly from churches, not through missionary organizations. So we are talking about thousands of people and lots of investment dollars.

Some people ask, and rightly so, why should we invest this way if we are not seeing large returns in short-term workers? Is this really a worthwhile investment? It's no hidden fact that over 15,000 missionaries are now retiring, or through death are going to be with the Lord. And right in the midst of a 10-year period when this is happening we are not even recruiting enough people to fill these gaps. And what about going to new groups of hidden peoples in the world; who will go? I believe that God is making His own investment through His Church, a people He is going to send out.

Short-term missionaries are our most valuable resource to fulfill a long-term mission vision. But I have to caution, we often want instant missionaries. We must first sow before we can reap. Dr. Ralph Winter has often told students they need to recruit others and share the vision before they go overseas. It's a slow, slow process. It does not happen overnight.

But we need not be negative. The dam will burst. I believe that God is going to send out thousands of young people in a way that He can be glorified. He will do it through prayer—prolonged prayer.

If we do not pray, God may either persecute us to get us moving or He may go around us to others to complete the task. Right now there are 15,000 to 20,000 young people in other cultures who are willing to go. They need money to go and adequate training. And somehow God is going to have these people go out and serve.

Now, how is a short-term missionary best prepared to take a step into long-term mission work? There are three non-negotiables: good training, good placement and an adequate re-entry program.

If you are looking at short-term missions or if you are counseling someone to be a short-term missionary, good training is a must. The missionary often becomes very "put-out" with short-term missionaries who come to the field and are not well-trained.

The second non-negotiable is good placement. If we counsel somebody to go to a Muslim culture who cannot handle that kind of situation emotionally, then we are not only stretching their faith but we may be hurting them for life. We need to consider their health and background before we encourage them to go to some difficult place.

The third non-negotiable is helping the short-term worker with their re-entry to the States. The veterans returning from Vietnam had re-entry problems. Many of them never talked about their problems. Now they have special centers all over the United States where they can come and talk. But generally there are no professionals to really help them work through what they experienced. The same is true of short-term missionaries.

These short-term missionaries are not out to have just some kind of an experience. They are on a mission. That is why we call them short-term *missionaries,* not short-term *workers.* And when they come back, they come back from the war. They have been in spiritual warfare. They have seen missionaries slap each other around verbally. They never expected that. They have seen the world's poorest people and are comparing this to how much we have in our country. They don't understand that. They need to be debriefed.

I believe it is the responsibility of church and mission leaders to provide good training, good placement and an adequate re-entry program.

Now there are four areas that are the responsibility of the short-termers. In Luke 2:52 it says, "Jesus increased in wisdom and in stature, and in favor with God and man" *(RSV)*.

As a short-term missionary, are you willing to grow? Are you willing to go through the pain of having your habits broken? A not-so-humorous note on this is about a fellow I saw when I was a missionary kid in the Philippines. He was a journeyman with the Southern Baptist, and he weighed about 250 pounds, a good-sized fellow. He came to the Philippians in the hot season and was to be there two years. Well, within a year, he returned to Manila from Northern Luzon. He had come down with what we called the "tropical trots." He went down to 125 pounds. As kids who didn't know better we laughed because this guy had really changed in appearance. The fact is, it was very painful, for the fellow was in desperate shape. Remember, as short-term missionaries go out they will encounter painful situations not of their choosing. Habits will have to be broken, values changed and attitudes altered.

Then as we look at short-term missions, we need to realize that Jesus Christ went through a growing process Himself. And as a short-term missionary you have to be willing to grow, even if it's painful. Short-term missions is not an end in itself, it is a means to an end. I like to say, as many of my fellow short-term leaders have said, "Short term missions is mobilizing God's people to do God's purposes here and around the world." It's just one step in a long process.

Third, we need to have a willingness to remove barriers ourselves. In going to Mexico City, my wife and I are faced with pollution, as are many people who go to urban areas. Mexico City has been said to be one of the most polluted cities in the world. The pollution is five times greater than what's considered the healthy breathing limit; it's just like smoking two packs of cigarettes a day.

Taking three kids to that environment, we have to really believe the safest place to be is in the center of God's will. We must believe that the will of God will not take us where the grace of God will not keep us. And God, through the Holy Spirit, has given us the inner strength to make decisions to break down the barriers that confront us.

The last responsibility of a short-termer is to expect different counsel when we return from overseas. Many people will say, "We need you here." And they are correct, we do have tremendous needs here. But we need to realize that if God has given us a good experience, and we have done well, then we should seriously consider work overseas. Quoting from the Student Volunteer Movement, "If it is a good thing to go where we are needed, is it not more Christlike to go where we are needed most?"

What is the responsibility of mission leaders? Leaders must spend their time not only doing today's ministry, but planning and equipping the short-term missionary who will return on a long-term basis. It is never convenient to counsel a short-term missionary to move long-term, but it's necessary to do so.

My staff found out one day how committed I was to this idea. A short-term missionary couple came back from Papua New Guinea. Now, they were not going to be going out with our organization, yet they were having lots of problems digesting everything that had happened to them over the last two years. So I closed the door to my office and told my staff not to disturb me. And I was there with that couple for three hours in the midst of much urgent work. We must do this sort of counseling in order to meet the needs of young people. If we don't meet them when they ask for it and when they are ready, the door of opportunity may close. So if you have the opportunity to help, take it.

For short-term missionaries, there are three verbs that can help guide us as to our responsibility. The first is *seek*. We must seek with all our heart to know what God would have us do, and not wait until we come back to the United States to do it. If we go out, we need to seek God about our future in the culture in which we are working, when we do not have a lot of the distractions of our society.

The second verb is *serve*. We must have a servant's heart. There are many passages throughout the Scriptures on the role of a servant. Matthew 23:1-12 and Luke 14:1-14 instruct us in this area. You might ask, "Why does God continue to repeat this?" It is because we are prone not to serve. If we go as a short-term missionary and do not serve, we will not have a good experience. We should never go if we are not willing to serve. I would like to share what I wrote after Loren Cunningham, founder of Youth with a Mission, and I spent some time together in Colorado. I wrote down in the back of my Bible: To serve I must set aside my rights, focusing my energy, status, and influence, however much, to raise up others on my team to be all that God wants them to be. Luke 22:26: "Let the greatest among you become as the youngest, and the leader as one who serves" (*RSV*).

Humility and servanthood go hand in hand. And the test of servanthood will be proven in standing the test of daily life with our fellowman. In our devotional life it's easy to think we are servants before God. But servanthood towards others will be the only sufficient proof that our servanthood before God is real. That servanthood has taken up its abode in us and has become our very nature so that we are actually more like Christ. What you and I are like in our unguarded moments, the common course of daily life, is the proving grounds for what is in our hearts.

The last verb is *sacrifice*. Yes, we must serve, but we must also sacrifice. I believe with all my heart that the sacrifices we are asked to make right now will be magnified so that many of us will lose our lives for the sake of Jesus Christ. Many of our children will die for Christ in years ahead. But I believe that is part of the life of a missionary.

In conclusion, we must have singleness of purpose, whether we go overseas two weeks, two years or a lifetime, remembering that we must introduce those who will outlive us to Jesus. Introduce them to the source of all good. Dr. A.T. Pierson of the Student Volunteer Movement said, "You have no right to hear and believe without testifying."

We need to pray: Our gracious God, we thank you so much for the privilege of serving you, specifically for those short-term missionaries that are serving career missionaries and Christian leaders in other countries around the world, that you might give them the heart of a servant and a heart of sacrifice. And then help them as they seek you and your church, as to their part in your great plan—not our plan, but your plan of world missions. We do love you. In Jesus' name. Amen.

13

Join a Concert of Prayer
by
David Bryant

I have an article by Robert E. Speer that was reprinted in the May-June 1986 issue of *World Christian* magazine. Speer was one of the earliest signers of the Student Volunteer Movement declaration and later became an influential missionary statesman.

In his article "The Secret of Endless Intercession" he writes, "Foreign work has been least fruitful when the church has prayed the least. The evangelization of the world in this generation depends on a revival of prayer. (Now, he's writing about his generation, but it's no less true for this generation.) Considering the fearful consequences of it, the current attitude of the church toward the power of prayer borders on criminal negligence. A far greater service or gift of eloquence, more desirable than gold, more to be sought than honor or opportunities is this gift, the secret of unceasing, prevailing, triumphant prayer for the coming kingdom of Jesus Christ. Seek the key to that secret. May God disclose it to us all."

Now that's the heritage we're celebrating: men and women like Speer who were Levites, who had such a vision for prayer for the world that they mobilized many others into prayer. And that's still happening today.

I received a phone call recently from the InterVarsity regional director in Birmingham, Alabama. He said, "David, I've got to share with you the tremendous thing that's happening here in Birmingham. It began a year ago. We now call it Birmingham Alive. Back last fall a group of 40 churches decided to hold 10 weeks of united prayer. We called them concerts of prayer. We met for a concert of prayer each week for 10 weeks. Two or three things have come out of that emphasis. First, God met us in a most unusual way and gave us such a vision for prayer, that now there are concerts of prayer going on all over the city.

"Second, God has given us a new understanding of what He would like to do to bring Christ and His Kingdom to the focus of attention within the life of our city— Birmingham Alive. Third, He's given us a vision for renewed efforts of church planting in Birmingham. Right now a number of denominations whose people are involved in this prayer movement in Birmingham are cooperating to bring in 22 church planters by the end of August. Those 22 church planters will have two responsibilities for the following 365 days. One, to do actual church planting. Second, to meet every single day of those 365 days with various members of the concerts of prayer in our city for two hours of prayer launching out that day to continue their tasks in church planting.

"Now," he said, "the reason I'm calling you is to see if I can get you down here to help us turn this thing full throttle toward a focus of prayer on *world* evangelization, so we can begin to see God answering our prayers by doing the same kinds of things in other parts of the world."

Well, there are prayer movements of that nature going on all over this country and all over the world. What thrills me is I know about so few of them because there's so much going on I can't keep track of it all.

Zechariah 8:20-23 best describes what a prayer movement for world evangelization is all about. It's a vision God gave through Zechariah to a little remnant of people who had come back to rebuild the Temple. After 70 years of captivity, they needed a vision to keep them at the work of rebuilding God's place of prayer. Here's what came to them:

> This is what the Lord Almighty says: "Many peoples and the inhabitants of many cities will yet come, and the inhabitants of one city will go to another and say, 'Let us go at once to entreat the Lord and seek the Lord Almighty. I myself am going." . . . In those days ten men from all languages and nations will take firm hold of one Jew by the hem of his robe, [that is, one of the praying people] and say, 'Let us go with you, because we have heard that God is with you'" *(NIV)*.

This was the theme passage for the International Prayer Assembly for World Evangelization (IPA) in 1984 when about 3,000 prayer leaders gathered not only to pray together but to think through strategies for mobilizing citywide and nationwide movements of prayer. We took Zechariah 8 as our theme passage and defined the theme for the IPA, "Seeking the face of God for a movement of prayer for the world." That is precisely what God is raising up at this hour. In many senses it is exactly what Zechariah says. It is one city literally going to another and saying, "Let us go at once."

We had a National Prayer Leader's Retreat in Chicago two months ago where some 70 leaders of citywide prayer movements in this country alone gathered together. For 48 hours we were locked up in a hotel together as we shared what God is doing, learned from one another how to serve our individual prayer movement better, and spent hours praying together that God would accelerate the work, not only in the cities we represented, but across our country.

The same thing is happening in other countries as well. In fact, The European Mission Association (TEMA) endeavor in Europe has set as its primary objective from Mission '87 in Holland to spawn concerts of prayer across Europe. Their strategy is this: The delegates will go back to their various nations and form prayer groups that will meet on a weekly basis. Then, once a quarter in a given country, and it's possible to do this on a national level in a country like the Netherlands, they will have a quarterly concert of prayer. Every quarter these little prayer groups will reconvene in a far larger night of united prayer for spiritual awakening and world evangelization. Talk about the center of work! So one city is calling another— literally—saying, "Come let us go at once."

Of course, it could be one Sunday School class calling another, or one individual calling another, or one InterVarsity chapter calling one Campus Crusade group on the same campus. But it must come with a conviction that says, I myself am going because it *must* take place, and it must take place at once.

The impact is that as God answers and makes His presence known among His people, two things happen: The gospel becomes *accessible* because many languages and nations are able to get at the praying people scattered abroad and say to them, "Take us with you," and second, the gospel becomes *credible*. The unconverted want to take hold of the messages in their midst and find out who

A Concert of Prayer provides visible expression of unity in the Body of Christ."

God is, because they can verify how He is tangibly and gloriously in the midst of His people. That's reverent! And that's the kind of prayer movement that is so critical to "the evangelization of the world in this generation."

I want to share a particular approach for a once a month gathering for a couple of hours, with people from a broad spectrum of the Christian community who usually aren't together under any other circumstances, maybe coming from different denominations or different campus groups. If they are from a particular campus, they may have different ways of praying, insights and views on various topics, all of which can be blended in a beautiful concert of people. We become like a symphony brought together under one conductor, the Lord Jesus, to play one score, the Bible. This is what a concert of prayer must do if we're going to play in unison and be a symphony together. This is our score. We must bring our prayers out of Scripture. Then despite our differences, we can all be sure we're on the right track and can truly agree with one another in the fullness of faith.

Concerts of prayer is a term widely used to define a distinctive prayer gathering, differing at a number of points from most other times Christians pray together. The distinctives suggest a different approach to how the prayer meeting is shaped and led. Here are *ten distinctives*, each of which comes into play in the practical format that follows:

One. A concert of prayer is marked by a *spirit of* celebration. Throughout we rejoice in hope, anticipating all God has promised to us in answer to our prayers for spiritual awakening and world evangelization.

Two. A concert of prayer *incorporates a broad scope* in what we pray for. Our focus is on two major Kingdom themes, like the treble and bass clef of a music score:

Fullness, revival or awakening in the Church and *Fulfill-ment,* the advancements of God's Kingdom in the world. The Lord's Prayer models both of these key concerns.

Three. A concert of prayer provides *visible expression of unity in the Body of Christ.* Like the variety of instru-ments in an orchestra, brought together under one Conductor—the Lord Jesus—to play from one score—the Scriptures, so believers united in prayer can release the music of God's Kingdom purposes for the whole world to hear. In a concert of prayer, Christians can experience at deep levels the unity Jesus intended (see John 17). Through corporate intercession we are newly forged to Christ, to each other and to Christ's mission in the world. While we may not yet be able to achieve visible unity in other areas, certainly we can and must do so in the arena of biblically grounded prayer, especially prayer for awak-ening and evangelization.

Four. A concert of prayer provides *a way to network the Body of Christ* within a city or on a campus. It helps us find one another across barriers, differences, spheres of influence and ministries that otherwise often divide us. It provides a neutral meeting ground. Here, despite our dif-ferences, the overarching Kingdom concerns that touch all of us can become our shared focus through united praying, and as a result, through joint-ministries (see Rom. 12:1-5, 11-13).

Five. Not only does a concert of prayer draw Chris-tians together from different spheres, *it also benefits Christians from all spheres.* The explanation is simple. When God answers Kingdom-sized prayers offered to Him unitedly, everyone in the prayer movement, plus the fel-lowships they represent, share together in being blessed (awakening) and in becoming a blessing to the families of the earth (world evangelization). God's whole vision for the whole city or campus (and, ultimately, beyond) must be realized through the whole Body. Thus, His answers are for the whole Body, too. A local concert of prayer may be the one ongoing effort among believers that foregoes any reasons for competition (see 1 Tim. 2:1-8).

Six. More specifically, a concert of prayer provides *a point of contact for praying people and prayer groups* within a city or on a campus. Here they can periodically interface, help each other expand their Kingdom concerns in prayer ministry within the fellowships from which they come, and take new faith and vision back into their ongoing prayer efforts day by day. Prayer leaders and prayer groups will come from at least three major parts of the Body: the church sphere, the missions sphere and the youth sphere. All three should be represented in a concert. Those from the *church* sphere bring strong nurturing concerns, which relate to revival; those from the *mission* sphere bring concerns for outreach and advancements; those from the *youth* sphere often carry fresh dreams and aspirations, as well as new leadership potential, for nurture and outreach ministries. We all need one another.

Seven. A concert of prayer also offers *a training ground for mobilizing prayer throughout the Body of Christ.* Through its regular impact on those who gather to pray, it naturally accelerates prayer and sharpens our prayer agenda everywhere within God's family. To help insure its contribution as a training ground, concerts should be sufficiently organized so that participants can adapt what they gain from the experience to use in the situations where they pray with others the rest of the month. Thus, a concert is both a *workshop* on prayer, as well as a ministry of prayer (see Luke 11:1). Along with the answers it secures from God's hand for the Church and the world, this training is another way prayer movements act as God's servants in the work of His Kingdom.

Eight. In addition to training in prayer, concerts of prayer provide *a sustaining foundation for ministry* both to the city or campus, and among the nations. It is a base of operations for advancing Christ's global cause as it: (a) equips the pray-ers to become more spiritually attuned servants; (b) helps the pray-ers to rededicate themselves to be Christ's ambassadors in any way He chooses; (c) plants in the hearts of the pray-ers new dreams and visions for ministry to earth's unloved and unreached; (d) attempts at times, to consciously link up the prayer movement with specific outreach efforts (evangelistic, justice, church-planting, etc.); (e) prepares the way for all other ministries inside and outside the Church as God goes ahead of us by actually answering our cries for spiritual awakening and world evangelization (see Ps. 65:1-8; Acts 13:1-4).

Nine. Historically, concerts of prayer have retained a sense of *manageability,* both in format and in frequency. Often in the past they have met once a month, allowing busy Christians to rearrange their schedules so that united prayer gets the priority it deserves. That way, those who participate, coming from different fellowships with differing responsibilities to those bodies, can still find a common time to gather without jeopardizing their other commitments. The same sensitivity is in evidence in prayer movements today.

Ten. A concert of prayer is more than an event. *It is a movement*—a process in which we are moving on from where things are (in us, in the Church, in the world) to where God desires and deserves things to be. We are involved in a long-term ministry, seeking long-term impact for the Kingdom through united prayer. This requires that those who join in be persevering servants, consistently involved on a regular basis and actively inviting others to join with them month by month (see Acts 1:14, 2:1,42; 4:23,24).

The following suggested format is only one model, but it does reflect many of the important distinctives found in concerts of prayer. You might think of it as training wheels on a child's bike. Without them it's hard to keep one's balance when you're just learning to ride. But once you have balance, all you need are the real wheels. Even so, it's up to each prayer group to decide when this format (training wheels) can be exchanged for other "wheels."

Format for a concert of prayer

1. Celebration (10 minutes)
   • Praise in hymns and choruses, focused on awakening and mission
   • Reports of God's answers to prayers offered up during previous concerts
   • Prayers of praise for God's faithfulness, for His Kingdom, for His Son

2. Preparation (20 minutes)
   • Welcome to the concert!
   • Overview: Why are we here?
   • Biblical perspectives on what we're praying toward (i.e. awakening, mission)
   • Preview of the format
   • Teaming-up in partners and in huddles

3. Dedication (5 minutes)
   • Commitment: to be servants through prayer and to

be used in answer to our prayers
- Thanksgiving: for the privilege of united prayer and for those with whom we unite
- Invitation for Christ to lead the concert and to pray through us
- Hymn of praise

4. Seeking for fullness/awakening in the Church (30 minutes)
   - In partners—for personal revival
   - In huddles—for awakening in our local churches and ministries
   - As a whole—for awakening in the Church worldwide
   - Pause to listen to our Father
   - Chorus

5. Seeking for fulfillment/mission among the nations (30 minutes)
   - In partners—for personal ministries
   - In huddles—for outreach and mission in our city
   - As a whole—for world evangelization
   - Pause to listen to our Father
   - Chorus

6. Testimonies: What has God said to us here? (10 minutes)
   - On fullness (awakening)
   - On fulfillment (mission)

7. Grand Finale (15 minutes)
   - Offering ourselves to be answers to our prayers and to live accordingly
   - Prayer for God's empowerment in our own lives for ministry

- Prayer for prayer movements locally and worldwide
- Offering praise to the Father who will answer our concert of prayer
- Leave to watch and serve "in concert"

Don't let the arbitrary time allotments be overly restrictive for you. On the one hand, order and timing are important to insure a balanced, in-depth coverage of the issues for which the movements exist. Further, some structure and control is required to insure a meaningful experience for the pray-ers, especially since they come from many backgrounds, and only meet periodically (once a month?).

But, we must also remain open to the Spirit's direction. Ultimately, it is Jesus, not a humanly devised format, who conducts each concert! Freedom and improvisation do have a place in God's Kingdom symphonies. So, we should pursue orderliness while, at the same time, we keep our eyes on the "Concert Master" for any adjustments He may want to make.

One nice feature of this particular format is that its basic components can be covered more briefly in a 30-minute gathering, or they can be expanded past two hours in order to provide a half-night of prayer (4 hours?). So, in the end, timing is up to the local prayer leaders and under the Spirit's guidance. However, many find that two hours are needed to give people a satisfying prayer experience. And people usually can't believe how swiftly two hours can pass in a prayer event of this nature!

Now, here are some comments on *the components* in the format. Each segment appears for a purpose. Experience has shown each to be essential in order to insure good coverage of the strategic issues for which the concert exists. Therefore, stress that pray-ers keep their thoughts relative to each component as you come to it. For example, urge that during the "fullness" segment, intercession should focus primarily on issues relating to awakening in the Church, while prayer for world needs can come later in the "fulfillment" segment.

Be sure to encourage everyone to work at maintaining a proper blend of *rejoicing, repenting* and *requesting* within segments, though the celebration component will be mostly rejoicing. Of course, the primary response experienced throughout all Concerts is this: *seeking* God's glory and Kingdom in Jesus Christ.

One final thought: This type of format can help you *put people at ease.* Coming from different backgrounds as we do, the format permits us to vary in our perspectives and ways of expressing ourselves in prayer, so as to make uniquely meaningful contributions to the whole concert thrust. Encourage everyone, however, to work at being sensitive to one another, neither offending nor judging one another, as we seek to pray in "harmony" and with singleness of purpose. Remind people to listen, build upon their prayers, and learn more from one another about how and what to pray.